The Aspie Girl's Guide to Being Safe with Men

of related interest

Making Sense of Sex
A Forthright Guide to Puberty, Sex and Relationships
for People with Asperger's Syndrome
Sarah Attwood
Illustrated by Jonathon Powell
ISBN 978 1 84310 374 5
eISBN 978 1 84642 797 8

Aspergirls
Empowering Females with Asperger Syndrome
Rudy Simone
Foreword by Liane Holliday Willey
ISBN 978 1 84905 826 1
eISBN 978 0 85700 289 1

Safety Skills for Asperger Women
How to Save a Perfectly Good Female Life
Liane Holliday Willey
Foreword by Tony Attwood
ISBN 978 1 84905 836 0
eISBN 978 0 85700 327 0

Asperger's Syndrome and Sexuality
From Adolescence through Adulthood
Isabelle Hénault
Foreword by Tony Attwood
ISBN 978 1 84310 189 5
eISBN 978 1 84642 235 5

THE
Aspie Girl's Guide to Being Safe *with* Men

The Unwritten Safety Rules
No-one is Telling You

DEBI BROWN

Foreword by Sarah Attwood

Jessica Kingsley *Publishers*
London and Philadelphia

Male and female genital diagrams on pp.79–80 from *Making Sense of Sex* by Sarah Attwood, published by Jessica Kingsley Publishers in 2008. Diagrams copyright © 2008 by Jonathan Powell. Reprinted with permission of Jonathan Powell.

First published in 2013
by Jessica Kingsley Publishers
116 Pentonville Road
London N1 9JB, UK
and
400 Market Street, Suite 400
Philadelphia, PA 19106, USA

www.jkp.com

Library of Congress Cataloging in Publication Data
Brown, Debi.
The aspie girl's guide to being safe with men / Debi Brown ; foreword by Sarah Attwood.
p. cm.
Includes bibliographical references and index.
ISBN 978-1-84905-354-9 (alk. paper)
1. Sex instruction for girls. 2. Asperger's syndrome. 3. Man-woman relationships. 4. Dating (Social customs) I. Title.
HQ51.B76 2012 646.7'7--dc23 2012027361

British Library Cataloguing in Publication Data
A CIP catalogue record for this book is available from the British Library

ISBN 978 1 84905 354 9
eISBN 978 0 85700 703 2

Printed and bound in Great Britain

For all Aspie girls and women everywhere,
hoping this will keep you safe

CONTENTS

Part 1: The Support, Knowledge and Skills You Need as Pre-requisites to Being Safe with Men

Part 2: Being Safe with Men: Protecting Yourself, Making Informed Choices and Acting on Your Choices

Foreword

During the many years I worked as a sexuality educator, I spoke to hundreds of parents of young children at kindergartens and preschools. One topic that always came up was that of sexual abuse, and how to protect young children. It is tempting to think that keeping our children in the house, only allowing them out under strict supervision, and teaching them about 'stranger danger' will minimise the possibility of their being singled out for sexual abuse. This, of course, is not the case. Over 80 per cent of child sexual abuse occurs within the home, perpetrated by a family member or friend.

So what is to be recommended? How can you protect young children from a threat that is potentially so close to home? Actually, it isn't all that difficult. The advice to parents is always:

Ensure that your child is able to name, using the correct terms, their private body parts.

Teach your child about privacy, and what this means in terms of private body parts, private places and private behaviours.

Communicate openly, lovingly and often with your child. Listen to them without judgement, so that they have the confidence to tell you whatever is on their mind.

Predators sniff out vulnerability. But a child who is demonstrably knowledgeable, secure and confident, and clearly has good communication with at least one adult in their life, is not vulnerable. A predator will give such a child a wide berth.

Debi Brown's book is not about young children. But it is about a vulnerable group of people, namely, Aspie girls and women. Their vulnerability stems from their social difficulties, where they may struggle to understand and be part of the social world. They may desperately want friends, yet find this difficult to achieve. They may be less knowledgeable about sexual facts than their peers, having missed out on the sharing of information that happens among teenagers. They may be willing to engage in sexual activity just to 'fit in', or in a mistaken attempt to boost their popularity or self-esteem. It is a disturbing fact that girls and women on the autism spectrum suffer more than their fair share of sexual abuse in childhood and adolescence, and abusive, dysfunctional relationships as adults.

As an Aspie herself, Debi Brown has written warmly, startlingly honestly and from a position of knowledge about how to address the problem of Aspie girls being safe in their relationships with men. She has understood the fundamental truth, that to ensure a girl's safety, it is vital to educate her. She needs to have a good knowledge of the real facts about sex; she needs to understand boundaries and what constitutes acceptable behaviour (both her own and her sexual partner's); and she needs a solid network of safe people to whom she can turn for advice and support. This is exactly the same framework as described above to protect children.

Debi doesn't use innuendo or assume knowledge on the part of the reader, since she has discovered through her own experience that these lead to misunderstandings. She takes you step-by-step through each stage, spelling out the facts, never mincing her words. She lays it bare, and when it all gets too difficult (some of the subject matter is deeply challenging), she envelops you warmly with reassurances and kind words. You feel as though you are sitting having a heart-to-heart chat with your best friend.

This beautifully written book should be essential reading for all young women, not just Aspies. It should certainly be read by anyone who loves and supports an Aspie. The themes that run through the book, of building up one's knowledge, learning about boundaries, developing friendship and relationship skills, and working towards a healthy independence and sexuality, are those that should be woven into the support that is given to every Aspie throughout their childhood, to provide the road map for a safe adult life.

Sarah Attwood
Author of Making Sense of Sex: A Forthright Guide to Puberty, Sex and Relationships for People with Asperger's Syndrome
August 2012

ACKNOWLEDGEMENTS

I would like to express my heartfelt gratitude to the following people for their help in connection with this book:

Charlene Tait and Scottish Autism, for immediately recognising the importance of this book and supporting it.

Jessica Kingsley Publishers, for publishing this book.

Stella Macdonald, for being a shining light and for continually showing me by her example that Aspies can do anything.

Lisa Clark, Camille Hayden and Susan Tullett, for reading the draft work and suggesting improvements.

Angèle Carruthers, for her encouragement and for pointing me in the direction of some things I did not know.

Sarah Attwood, for educating me in a major and always gentle way, and for copy-editing the book and writing the Foreword.

Jonathon Powell, for allowing me to use his drawings.

Sinead Feeney, for outstanding courage and friendship above and beyond the call of duty.

Fiona Merriweather, for a heart-debt that can never be repaid and without whom this book could never have been written.

DISCLAIMER

I am writing from my position as an Aspie who has made mistakes. I am not a doctor or any other kind of medical professional. Much of what I have found out is therefore by my own research, and I have referenced my sources, but the information can only be as good as the sources. I have tried to do my research diligently, and every effort has been made to ensure that the information contained in this book is correct, but I have not written this book from any point of high wisdom on the topics. I have written this because I could see what is missing in the general education of Aspie girls and women, and because I believed that I knew how to write it in a way that would be understandable and clear and, I hope, fill in some of the gaps. Some of this information is a matter of life and death. None of the information contained within this book is to be taken as medical advice. This book is intended as preliminary reading material to help you to be aware of the important issues. Always consult with your doctor and make sure that you do your own research to verify both what I have said here and your own understanding of it.

WHY I WROTE THE ASPIE GIRL'S GUIDE AND WHY YOU SHOULD READ IT

I wrote *The Aspie Girl's Guide* because it had to be written.

I wrote *The Aspie Girl's Guide* because many Aspie girls and women are getting raped, and many others are getting sexually abused or forced into situations they do not want or understand. I did not particularly want to write it, and if you had told me a year ago that I would be writing something like this, I would have told you that you were crazy. It was excruciating to write. I have written things that I am so uncomfortable and embarrassed about that I cannot say them out loud, and even having the people I trust most reading the first draft was a horrifying experience. (It was also quite funny as I found myself literally shrinking down in my seat and trying my best to hide behind a book I was holding at the time, which of course did not really work.) I have the feeling that quite a few other people *could* have written this book, but no-one yet has, because it hurts too much and it costs too much to do it.

I started to write this book after reading in the newspaper about a 16-year-old Aspie girl who had been raped by her special needs teacher over a period of two years. He locked her in the classroom and in a cupboard. He told her this was what she wanted, and I guess she must have believed him. I was shocked and I wondered how anyone could be taken in like that. Then I remembered something that had happened to me when I was 19, which I had completely suppressed to the extent I had actually forgotten it entirely. When I remembered it, I was re-traumatised all over again and I had to get help to deal with it. In trying to figure out where I had gone wrong (and in trying to explain why I was not, perhaps contrary to appearances, a total slut), I found a lot of things that I had completely misunderstood, and I found myself saying, 'When there is information, it is never clear enough.' A few days later, feeling a lot better, I started to realise that I could now write something that was, in fact, clear enough.

In a recent discussion around this topic, I learned to my astonishment that a lot of people get their sex education and learn how to deal safely with men as teenagers, via conversations in the playground at secondary school. What sort of system of knowledge transfer is that? *A cultural knowledge system reliant on folks having good social networks is not a fair system and is not going to work for most Aspie girls. This is a selfish system, which puts more weight on appearances and not embarrassing people who would rather not give explicit information than it does upon keeping girls and women safe.* This book is about 55,000 words long and I am struggling not to make it longer. In no other area of life important to our safety and well-being would we be expected to acquire 55,000 words' worth of knowledge without being taught. This is utterly ridiculous and it is not acceptable.

As children and teenagers, we Aspie girls are much less likely to have the close-knit social links with our peers that would get us this very information we need to be safe. When we are adults, we are much more likely to have these supportive links, but who is going to take aside their (possibly undiagnosed) 25-year-old Aspie friend, or 42-year-old Aspie friend, and say, 'Excuse me, do you want me to teach you about men and sex and stuff and how to avoid dangerous situations?' By then, it is assumed knowledge, and it would highly embarrass most adults to do this. From our side, we Aspies can usually communicate extremely well if we realise (a) the need to communicate, (b) what we need to communicate, and (c) what we do not already know that we need to know. But the problem comes if we do not realise the need to communicate, or the need for more (or better) information than we have. *The Aspie Girl's Guide* aims to give important and relevant information to people who may not even realise they need it or that they are lacking any of it.

I have been lucky. The thing that happened to me was not world-shatteringly bad, although it was certainly bad enough. But it was still traumatising. I am very lucky now that I found someone I could tell it all to and get de-traumatised from it. We need information about what to do if the worst happens, because it sometimes will, even if we get everything right. No-one's safety is guaranteed. This book will not be easy reading. But it is necessary and I have tried to write it in a very friendly, straightforward and loving style so it is as painless as possible. Some of the subject matter is scary and potentially upsetting, but I believe that ultimately, although reading the information might hurt a bit, *not* having the information will hurt a lot. I would rather read about something difficult than learn, unprepared, through experience. We need the facts, even about the bad stuff. Ultimately, nothing hurts so much as not having them. The truth is always the best way.

The Aspie Girl's Guide needs to be read, *especially* by Aspie girls and women who are not all that interested or motivated to have relationships and have sex, because these Aspies may think they do not need to know this stuff, whereas actually everyone needs to know it. My book needs to reach people who would not go to the bookshelves looking for books on sex.

Some of what I have written is information that I did need but that I did not get: not from my parents, not from my teachers, not from my friends, not from books; not from anywhere. If even intelligent, capable and lucky people like me are slipping through the cracks, not getting the knowledge we need to be safe, both physically and emotionally, then what on earth is happening to everyone else?

Introduction

I want to start by saying that I realise you might not be very willing to read this. I would not have been, if I were you. It partly concerns sex and men and all sorts of stuff that confuses me, embarrasses me, and much of the time, I would like to stay far away from. If it makes you feel any better, I am feeling probably just as unwilling to write it. But it is better to read this now and be prepared, than to learn by experience in potentially dangerous situations. There is also some stuff in here that is just good to know for life in general.

I am an Aspie. I have written about some situations that I have been in and others that I have not, some that are innocent and others that are abusive. I hope, in your life, you will only have good experiences and none of the bad ones. I just want you to know what the rules are and what could potentially happen; and I want you to have enough knowledge to be as safe as possible out in the world.

I have generally felt pretty uninterested in many of the topics that we are going to look at in this book and, as a result, I have not learned anything about them. However, I have realised that actually, none of us can afford to be uninterested because these things concern our safety and well-being. And just because we do not plan on doing something or being in a certain situation, other people have their own plans for us, so we really do have to be informed. It is always good to have knowledge that will keep you safe. In a strange way, I now feel more secure having researched some of the bad situations because I now feel like I would know a bit more what to do if I get into one in the future. And that is comforting. I hope you will find this too.

I really do recognise how potentially scary some of the topics covered by this book might feel – especially to Aspies because we are really sensitive. This is especially so if you are young, physically or emotionally, and most especially if you have already had some bad sexual experiences in your life – reading this could trigger you to remember them. However, avoiding scary topics is not always a good idea. If you are feeling scared or disturbed about some bits of this, take it slowly and do not try to read too much at once. When I deal with something scary, I like to take breaks and do something that makes me feel really safe in the breaks – in my case, usually something quite childish. What you want to do is to avoid over-thinking on the scary topics. Spending time with other people or a pet can be a great distraction from this. You might want to discuss some of these topics with someone else – for example, a parent, or someone who is like a parent to you. What you would need here is someone very sweet, very lovely, very wise and very safe. The good news is, as you get more used to the scary bits, your tolerance will increase and you will become more capable of dealing with them. That was certainly my experience.

Some people behave well and some people behave badly. Really bad behaviour is called abuse. Abuse can be physical (for example, someone kicking you), emotional (for example, someone telling you that you are worthless) or sexual (for example, someone forcing you to have sex with them against your will). Neglect of children by their parents (or other caretakers) is also a form of abuse.

Most men are good and will never do any of these things. Some men are largely good, but behave badly when it comes to women/girls. Some men do tend to want sex more than women and this does not, in itself, make them bad. Therefore, not every situation that you might want to avoid is caused by someone else being bad, although some situations might be. I hope it will be clear from what I have written which situations are bad and abusive and which are with good people, where some knowledge beforehand and some good communication will keep you safe.

Every girl and woman is potentially vulnerable to bad men. However, Aspie girls and women can be more vulnerable than most people, because:

- we can have difficulty telling a good person from a bad one

- we might have difficulty interpreting facial expressions

- we might find it hard to know if we are being lied to

- we might seek out quiet places (for example, alleys and parks at night) because we like the quiet and we want to avoid sensory overload – but these quiet places are where bad people might be waiting

- we are overwhelmed a lot of the time with too much information to process in every instant of our lives, so we can be slower to work things out

- we might not automatically know how to act in social situations

- we might not understand when someone does something wrong to us

- if we do know that someone is doing something wrong to us, we might not know how to stop it

- a lot of what we really need to know are 'unwritten rules', which non-spectrum people may find intuitively obvious without their ever being told them, but which we do need to be taught. If we have not been lucky enough to know the right people, perhaps no-one has ever taught us, or no-one has taught us in the right way

- although there are many more good men than bad men in the world, the bad men are very good at spotting that we Aspies are extra-vulnerable. They might not spot that we are Aspies. But they can spot that we are innocent and trusting and not so able to protect ourselves as other people. Bad men might make us their target, because they think that we will be easy to deceive and that they will get away with whatever they want to do with us.

On the plus side, we Aspies *are* very good learners if we can get the information explained to us properly, and this is what I have tried to do here. This is my attempt to write down some of the many unwritten rules, so that they are, in fact, written for you. So, it is very important that you read this.

As a good, typical Aspie, I love rules, I love certainty and I can have very black and white thinking at times. I feel so tempted to write this book as a rule book and tell you exactly what to do and what not to do, according to my personal opinions and beliefs. It would probably be clearer for you if I did this, but it would not be very good for you. My opinions are not necessarily 'right' because often, I regret to say, there is no right answer, which is what makes the whole thing so very confusing, not only for us but for the entire non-spectrum population too. You will find a few of my opinions in here, but I have tried to restrain myself in general, and you do not have to agree with me. Dating, sex and all this stuff is in the realm of social interaction, which is not very much based on logic and there is a lot of free choice in it. I *will* be very clear sometimes when I am talking about abusive situations that you *must* do something or other. However, when I am talking about non-abusive situations, where some parts of society choose one thing and some another, I cannot tell you what to do and you have to choose for yourself. These choices are yours to make and not mine to make for you. If you need help to decide, you can do some further research to get more information and you can discuss this with safe people in your life.

Not having had a book like this one to read myself, or any effective education on these topics that was clear enough for me to understand, I have made some very ill-informed decisions in the past. So, my aim in writing this is to give you enough information so that you can make your own better and more informed decisions.

I also need to briefly mention what this book is not. In writing this, I have tried to stick to my title – *The Aspie Girl's Guide to Being Safe with Men*. Therefore, this is not an instruction book on how to do sex or relationships – the emphasis is much more on being safe. Likewise, this book does not cover gay relationships and activities. Some people are gay. This means that some women have sex with other women and some men have sex with other men. I think this is completely fine, provided that this is between two consenting, loving adults, but these situations are not covered by the title and are therefore not included.

However, I do need to point out that behaving in a good or evil way is a choice that every individual has. Women can choose to behave badly, just as men can – for example, by being emotionally, physically and/or sexually abusive.

Thankfully this is rare, but mothers and/or fathers can even abuse their own children. Loving parents will love you unconditionally, no matter what you do, what you do not do, how many mistakes you make, and no matter who you are, Aspie or not, and they would never hurt their child on purpose. However, abusive parents can abuse their own children, or stand by passively and allow someone else to abuse them. This could be for many different reasons. Some abusive parents were abused themselves, when they were children. Some people are just evil. Some people are incapable of love. Some people are so damaged themselves that they fail to do the right thing to protect their children. Some people are terrible parents, either wilfully or incompetently. Parents are not automatically right or good simply because they are parents.

Hence, because of the title, this book does not deal directly with women abusers or maternal abusers, although these are also incredibly important topics. Just be aware that abuse by women can also happen, and these are topics in which you can do your own additional research, if needed. However, a lot of the knowledge in this book is directly transferable to these other situations, because what to do about it is the same, regardless of who you are with. You need these safety skills to be safe in all relationships, not just ones with men.

PART I

The Support, Knowledge and Skills You Need as Pre-requisites to Being Safe with Men

CHAPTER I

Your Support Network

What is your support network?

Okay, this may seem a funny sort of place to start, but actually, relationships and men are very confusing things and everyone, no matter who they are, Aspie or otherwise, will need some help in this area. This is one of the things your support network is for.

Your support network is made up of your safe people. A safe person is someone who you can trust 100 per cent. It is someone you can be honest with. It is someone who is accepting of you and not judgemental. It is someone who will not reject you, no matter what you tell them. It is someone who does not lie to you or manipulate you. It is someone who can understand you. It is someone who will not be using you for their own gain. It is someone highly moral. It is someone whose judgement you can trust and who is often right about things. It does not matter hugely where you find these people. Just find them, recognise them, build yourself a little team of them, and use them when you find yourself in a confusing situation, when you need information and when you are not sure what to do.

It is important to have a range of people in your support network. These can include friends, family, people at work, professionals and other Aspies. The more varied, the better. Try to ensure that your support network does not rely exclusively on professionals that are being paid to support you. It is fantastic if you have such professionals in your life, but you also need to know that some of your support people help you just because they love you. This is harder with professionals as, however kind, good, capable and brilliant at understanding you they are, they are getting paid to do it and they need to maintain a professional–service user distance. So, whilst in one sense, it is much easier to have trained professionals (they are already trained, available, understanding and they do not require anything back from you), you also really need people who love and value you for you, without any external commitment to you or their employer. This requires much more proactive behaviour on your part, together with better planning and relating skills, but is definitely worth the effort. Your support network is not something that is going to be given to you – you will have to make it for yourself.

The non-spectrum world uses such networks a lot and I think this is how a lot of unwritten rules get spread around and learned by non-spectrum people. I do not find it comes so naturally to ask people for advice, especially when I feel really sure I already know the answer, and especially when I am totally embarrassed by even the mention of the topic of boyfriends. However, I am finding that I can get things about men really wrong, and it is important to find out the facts.

Support networks in general can include both men and women. But for questions related to boyfriends and sex, you may want to pick a woman out of your support network to discuss this with. Yes, it is hugely embarrassing. But this is a matter of your safety, which is so much more important than your embarrassment. And if you have chosen your safe person well then, scary as it still is, you are not really risking anything, as your safe person will not reject you.

If you are hugely embarrassed about having to communicate something, here are two ideas that can make it easier:

1. Write it down instead of saying it – for example, in an e-mail, or write it on paper and give it to the person. Actually, writing is the most obvious example, but any way of making the communication more indirect seems to help. When I am embarrassed, I find it easier to say something by touch than with words. I am less embarrassed to say something in French than in English.

2. Say it, but find a way that means you do not have to make eye contact or see the other person's face when saying it. This helps a lot. You can pretend to yourself they are not really there and hearing it. You cannot see their facial expression, so this removes a visual stimulus and all visual clues as to what they may be thinking. Just switch off any thoughts and awareness

of how they might be reacting to what you are saying, and concentrate entirely on the difficult job of saying it. Use your Aspie hyper-focus skills to help you here.

What makes a good support person?

This section will explain the personal qualities that I look for in the people I choose to be my support people.

A miniscule number of people deal with me perfectly, instinctively, without effort and without any learning. Another group of people are just not capable of relating to me at all and never will be. A further group of people might not be great at first, but can learn a lot and improve; I can train them. Communicating as an Aspie, with anyone, involves a phenomenal amount of effort and a phenomenal amount of words. I am sometimes exhausted by all the explaining I have to do over the simplest of things. Sometimes, just in one situation, there are sensory issues, dyspraxia, not understanding what to communicate and communicating in the wrong way, all having effects that need to be explained. The full answer to one question might be nine pages of handwriting. With the miniscule number of people who just 'get me', it is lovely because slightly fewer words are needed. But even so, it is still a lot of words and effort. The effort is worth making though, because there are massive rewards in terms of having people in your life who actually understand you. I talk most to the people who understand me the best.

Fundamentally, I am looking for someone who genuinely likes me/loves me. This can be difficult to work out unless people are very clear, since kindness from others can look so like genuine love when it might not actually be that. For example, if someone is a professional, they may be kind to me mostly because it is their job to help me. Equally, I can get it wrong in the other direction: I can assume someone is being nice to me just because they are pitying me or being charitable, whereas they might actually love me and I do not know it. I sometimes figure it out eventually, but it really helps if people are clear about how they feel about me and what our relationship means to them.

I look for support people who are happy and well balanced in themselves. Damaged souls do further damage when they rub up against other damaged souls and Aspies are very likely to have damaged souls – not forever, but at least as a starting point to work with. If anyone is damaged, some of their own self-protection mechanisms can get in the way of helping us as they would really like to. This happens to me too, when I am trying to help others. When some of my damaged bits get a bit more healed up and I am more secure in myself, I will be more effective at helping others.

I very much need someone who is not judgemental or critical. Aspies are extremely sensitive to criticism. Our motives are often misunderstood – our outward appearances often do not match the inner truth. I have a lot of wounds of rejection from my past, and people who criticise me in anything but the most loving and gentle way trigger all the pain from these past experiences. I find this very difficult to cope with: I feel further rejected and damaged.

I need someone who never starts any sentences with the words, 'Because you have autism, you cannot…' Also, any sentences starting 'You cannot…' when talking about our abilities are very damaging. Being diagnosed with autism can be a devastating thing if not handled in the right way. I read about all the appalling statistics for adult life (which cannot actually be indicative of the whole population because of the vast quantities of non-diagnosed people who are doing well and living just fine). I read about impairments, cognitive deficits and brain lesions. I immediately started to think I was far less capable than I am and that my future was doomed. Actually, autism does not make anything impossible, so the 'you cannot' part is not true. It just makes some things much harder. I need to get out of my head all the 'you cannots' that are already there. Anyone adding more 'cannots' incurs my wrath! I might not be able to tell them this (that involves a quick response and assertiveness skills that I am still working on and practising), but I am cowering away from them inside and hurting very much.

I look for people who will take the time to get to know me and listen to me (even if I do tend to go on a bit!). I need someone who does not assume that all autism stereotypes apply to me. What people commonly assume is that I do not live independently, that I cannot understand basic expressions such as 'hanging around' or 'he laughed his head off', that I never understand sarcasm and that I cannot read facial expressions at all, to any extent. None of this is actually true.

I need someone who will care enough to bother to ask me embarrassing questions (such as 'Have you ever had a boyfriend?'). I am not good at realising what I need to communicate, so someone who can ask the right questions can sometimes tease out really important information that I would never have disclosed otherwise.

I need someone very encouraging and affirming. When I think about the people I love the most, there is a very strong link between how much I love the person and how encouraging they are. My favourite people tell me that I am worth a lot, that I am very precious, special and rare and that I am a blessing to them and a good person for them to have in their lives. Aspies tend to get a lot of feedback about how we are getting things wrong and we certainly experience getting things wrong a lot. What we get frequently over our entire lives, from early childhood onwards, is feedback from others that we are too slow, too stupid, too selfish, too naive, too poor at communicating, too weird, too wrong, that we do not fit in, that we are inferior to everyone else and that our place is at the bottom of every social hierarchy. This may cause us to have thoughts that we are worthless, that we are certainly worth less than everyone else, and that we are bad and defective people – in other words, really low self-esteem. But in the same way that damage is done by nasty words, healing is also done by kind words of love. The angle of the vector is the same, but the arrow of the vector is pointing in the opposite direction.

Our support people can help so much by encouraging us and praising what is good about us and what we do. I cannot stress highly enough the importance of doing this and the effect it can have deep within the Aspie soul. Low self-esteem and negative self-beliefs do not change overnight, because we are often up against a mountain of all the bad stuff. But if our support people just keep plugging away, drip, drip, dripping in the positive, over time, they will massively help us change our negative self-beliefs. Western society is not good at positive feedback to others, so being very positive and encouraging is a skill that might need some practice. Our support people can point out some of our good qualities (how much joy we have in life, how good we are with kids, how brave we are, how honest we are). Even if all that is seen is only the tiniest bit of good ('Thank you for making me a cup of tea, you are a good host'), they can praise it and we will be nurtured and start to flourish. This is also a two-way street; everyone (Aspie or not) needs encouragement, and we can be encouraging and a blessing to others, too.

Most of my life experiences have taught me that being different to others is a very bad thing. Being different sometimes gets me rejected, mocked and excluded; it gets me funny looks, it gets people to laugh *at* me rather than *with* me, it even sometimes gets me mocked or sneered at by strangers in the street. In the world, being different is not safe. Humans are tribal and everyone is concerned about being the same as everyone else. However, the belief that it is bad to be different to others is unhelpful, because I am really quite different to most people, so this belief encourages me to hate myself. So it is particularly great when my support people feed into my head that being different is a good thing, and that I am different in many wonderful ways.

It is especially wonderful when someone tells me that they appreciate my Aspie qualities, and tells me what they value and why. We can be tempted to hate our Aspie features because of the problems that can arise, because of how vulnerable we are and because these seem to be what make it so hard for us to make friends or be accepted. If anyone tells me they wish that non-spectrum people could become a bit more like me, I will love them forever!

I particularly look for someone who is honest, genuine, brave and not scared to be different themselves. Very special Aspies and non-Aspies can be all these things. A person worried about *themselves* seeming socially normal is not going to manage to help me in the way that I need to be helped. For example, I am emotionally still pretty young, although I am technically an adult. Emotionally, I think I might be around age 12 and, particularly when I am scared or upset, I often need exactly what a 12-year-old would need. Often, what I most need is a parent – not necessarily my actual parents, but support people who take on that role. I have about five 'parents' at the moment. I really need them and they are some of the most important people in my life. I also really need them to not demand that I act like an adult all the time. Life has never seemed safe. I need to feel safe as a child before I can grow up properly into an adult. If people provide this safety and support, I will love them. Some of the things I need my 'parents' for are advice when I have to make difficult decisions, and for emotional support when I am upset. I also need them to stay calm when I am upset.

Some Aspies may not have some of the close personal relationships that some other people do have. I do not have a boyfriend, a husband or children and I live by myself. But everyone needs hugs and physical contact. The people I like best are ones that give me hugs.

I need someone very, very gentle all over, with their words, with their touch, with their actions, with the loudness of their voice. I need to trust them when my world is falling apart, my thoughts are out of control and when my heart is in a thousand tiny pieces. If people go round speaking in very loud voices and waving their bodies around chaotically, I will back away from them very quickly. I will never learn how nice they are, because I will not get within five feet of them.

People who have children of their own have a big advantage when it comes to being a support person. Many things that apply to their children (for example, the knowledge that if you promise a six-year-old something, you must do it) apply equally for Aspies. Simple explanations for children work well for Aspies.

I need someone who is good at helping me process my emotions. I believe the root difficulty that causes so many of the other Aspie characteristics is an information processing problem: the total bandwidth for processing everything (thoughts, emotions, hunger, cold, sensory information, body signals) is far too small. I tend to prioritise thoughts, but all these other things get neglected and I do not process them much, particularly in social interactions, when I am already thinking on overdrive. If my support people can see my face, they might be able to tell from my facial expression what my emotion is or if I am cold. They might know this long before I do (if I ever know it). I sometimes need people to tell me what I am feeling. Sometimes, all I know is that I feel really screwed up but I do not know why. I sometimes need people to tell me why I am feeling it – for example, 'You might be feeling upset because you just took a big risk earlier today by telling me what you did, and now you could be feeling vulnerable and exposed.'

I need someone who does not take offence when I tell them something they already know (which I do a lot, due to not being sure of what they know) and who will not think I am patronising them. I need people who do not assume a reason for my behaviour, but instead ask me what the reason is.

Personally, I need someone both highly intelligent and highly empathic. Without high intelligence, the person is likely to get stuck in all the aspects where I am not the same as them, and the explanations get exhausting and unsatisfying because there may ultimately still be no understanding. Without high empathy, disclosing anything that makes me vulnerable is risky because I have a high chance of getting hurt by the response. People often hurt each other accidentally – much more often than on purpose, in my experience. However, just because it is accidental does not mean that it is not damaging.

I like someone who will be both interested and capable of understanding when I explain things about being an Aspie, and someone interested in learning about this.

I look for people who are good at teaching and explaining things; who do not assume lots of knowledge, but who start from the basics. Usually the communication error that non-spectrum people make is starting from step 7 (assuming steps 1 to 6 are known) rather than step 1.

I need someone who accepts that I am an Aspie, and who does not think this is a disease to be either cured, denied or hidden by pretending to be normal. I will always learn and improve, but I fundamentally need someone who does not want to change me but values me as I am. Pretending is a useful skill for certain situations, but it comes at a high cost, and if I have to do it all the time, I hate it and I hate myself. No-one will ever be close to me when I am pretending, because no-one can even have a glimpse of who I really am. No-one can feel love through a mask. No-one can be loved through a mask, because even if you are appreciated, what is being appreciated is the mask, which is fake.

I need someone who sees it as their responsibility to adapt to me as much as it is my responsibility to adapt to them. The adaptions should be equal, rather than it being entirely my job to act more like a non-spectrum person and conform to the 'right way' of doing things. Likewise, I like people who realise they have as much to learn from me as I have from them – not someone who just sees themself as the helper and imparter of all knowledge to the Aspie. We need our relationships to be reciprocal in some way, and for this to be recognised and acknowledged. We need to be valuable to other people and not objects of pity.

In summary, a support person has as many as possible of the following qualities. A good support person:

- understands me

- genuinely likes or loves me, and is happy to tell me this
- is happy and well balanced
- is not judgemental or critical
- believes in me and my abilities
- does not assume I am an autism 'stereotype'
- can talk openly and frankly with me, and encourages me to do the same
- is encouraging and affirming
- appreciates my differences and my Aspie qualities, and values me as I am
- is not scared to be different
- can be a 'parent' to me (and perhaps has children of their own)
- gives me hugs and physical contact
- is altogether gentle (with their words, touch, actions and voice)
- can help me process my emotions
- is both intelligent and empathic
- is a good teacher and communicator, who does not necessarily assume knowledge on my part
- is prepared to engage in a respectful, reciprocal relationship with me.

Note to support people

If you get even some of this stuff right, you will be very precious to us. Probably a lot more precious to us than we are to you. We might not know how to repay your kindness. We may not know how to meet your emotional needs. We might really like you and appreciate you, but not realise that we should communicate this to you in any way. We might eventually catch on and understand a little bit of what you need emotionally from us, but it could take us years.

I learn social stuff in the same way that I teach myself ice-skating. I do a thousand wobbly spins on one foot, and on one of them, I notice I was accidentally more stable when I tilted my foot further onto the edge of the blade. I then do this in future attempts. I did not know at the start that this would happen – but I just tilted my foot as part of the one thousand variations in trial and error. In the social arena, occasionally I say just the right thing, act in a way I have never acted before or I just happen to observe something I have never noticed before which informs how I act. I did not really understand it, I did not work it out, and even trying it was a leap of faith, but it seems to have a good result, so I can repeat it. This is not the same as intuitively having Theory of Mind, or understanding other people's thoughts and feelings. This is random trial and error. This is how I learn. Most of us do not intuitively and instinctively know how to meet other people's emotional needs, so until we have learned to do this, it is unlikely that we will meet them by accident. Since people mostly only like other people who *do* meet their emotional needs, this can lead to isolation.

I guess that means that you need to give to us, certainly at first, without expecting anything back, because it is quite probable that you will not get anything back. Not because we do not want to, but because we might not have figured out how to do it. I remember feeling astonished to find out that I could be a blessing to anyone else. You could, however, point us to some books or teach us what you need by telling us. Hopefully we will eventually catch on and start reflecting back to you what you give us. What happened with me was that someone was so incredibly nice to me, over a long period of time, that it eventually reached a tipping point where I was just so grateful that it demanded an emotional response back from me. I was very scared of giving this and did not really know how to, but I could not help doing so anyway.

How to make your own support network

I really do believe that we know who we need as our support people when we meet them. They do not pick us, *we* pick *them*! And they know when they have been picked…

People who are instinctively brilliant with us are very, very rare. So, if you find one, do not worry about where you find them (the supermarket, your work, your church, your dance class, your first aid course, at the swimming pool, etc.), just try to keep them because they are not replaceable.

Here are some ideas of what to do that might help you meet people; the more people you meet, the more likely you are to find the special ones with the qualities you are looking for:

- Join clubs and you can meet people with the same special interest as you. Clubs often have the advantage of weekly meetings that fit wonderfully into a routine and require very little ongoing planning or social arranging once the routine is established. Hence, clubs can help both loneliness and a need for structure and routine – result!

- Join a community that meets together at least once per week and take part wholeheartedly.

- Make friends with your friends' children. A lot of us are naturally good at this and really enjoy that anyway. A bonus is that their parents might also parent you a bit, and they might turn out to be great support network people.

- Share a flat.

- Get a routine that involves as much social activity as you need to be happy and joyful and try to have one exciting and social thing each day that you really look forward to.

- Accept social invitations.

- Join an autism social group/activity group and make friends with other Aspies. Not all Aspies and not all friends are suitable support network people though, and you may have to figure out what you are safe to tell to whom. 'Support network people' and 'friends' are two different categories of people who you need to deal with in different ways. Support network people need to be really stable in themselves – otherwise you will just spike up against each other when your self-protective spikes hit their emotional wounds, and vice versa, which can hurt very much indeed.

- Be brave, no matter how many times you have been rejected in the past. You will not find a support network in your home – you need to go out and interact.

- Volunteering is a good activity; it is fun and social, it boosts self-esteem, it is a means of giving to others and also, you might find some good support network people in your co-volunteers.

Here are some ideas of what you can do when relating to people, which might give them reasons to like you:

- Be friendly and a bit extrovert.

- Use your funny stories to make people laugh. Being an Aspie is an endless source of comic situations. I have figured out who will like to hear about these and I remember the stories until I see them next.

- Play to your strengths and use your uniqueness and difference as a way of appealing to others. You can tell people things they will not hear about from anyone else. You can love them in a way that will be completely different to anyone else.

- Trust people who you like and allow them to get close to you and to know the real you. This is risky stuff and I find it scary (because I sometimes feel afraid that the real me might not be lovable), but choose your people wisely and the actual risk is small, although the fear may still be great. Build up trust slowly; start with little things, and if your trust is honoured, move on to more difficult things. The payoff is finding out that the real you is very lovable – and that is invaluable.

- Get emotionally healed up as much as you can. Then you will be less spiky in your dealings with others.

- Remember that saying negative things is risky. I have never offended anyone by being positive but I have by being negative. You cannot be positive all the time, and I am not recommending that you lie, but what you say, when and to whom needs to be carefully judged. And you do not want to be seen to be the person who is always moaning or focusing on the negatives.

- If you like/love someone, tell them.

- Get good at giving people words of encouragement and be genuine about it. Everyone really needs this. They might even love you back. This may not come at all naturally (it is not what our society does), but Aspies are good with words and we can learn to do this really well.

- Reach out to people – make the first move. This is against all my instincts, but if you are only ever passive, people are unlikely to reach out to you.

- Learn about psychology, learn about non-spectrum people, learn about what other people need emotionally and do these things. Things that generally make other people feel good emotionally include physical touch, compliments/words of encouragement, quality time, acts of service and gifts. An excellent book on this topic is *The Five Love Languages* by Gary Chapman (1992). This is a Christian book, but no belief or religion is required in order to understand or apply the concept of giving love in these five particular ways. I strongly believe this book is equally applicable to people of all faiths and none. I think this idea is absolutely brilliant for Aspies, because these are five simple things that you can do for other people even if you are not sure how they are feeling. No mind-reading abilities are required!

The value of community

I believe that the ultimate solution is to be found in community rather than in the autism services. It is about being deeply embedded in a network of real-life relationships which are numerous and strong enough to make you safe and protected, with all your differences, strengths and vulnerabilities.

I feel part of a community at my church. I get a lot of emotional support there, which has the advantage that it is long term and not reliant on government funding, which can so easily, abruptly and devastatingly be withdrawn. I also feel secure in receiving their help because they are not getting paid for it.

By 'community', however, I do not just mean being part of a pre-existing social structure like a church community; it is helpful to have something like this but it is not the only way and is not the entire answer. Simply joining a community is not enough, because you still have to interact and make your own relationships within it. By 'community', I mean being part of a spider's web of relationships with other people. Community means having connections with others; the good news is that you *can* get and nurture these connections.

CHAPTER 2

Boundaries

What are boundaries?

Boundaries define limits and can be either visible or invisible. A kerb is an example of a visible boundary, and defines what is the pavement and what is the road. Other boundaries are invisible, but are just as important. Boundaries define what is 'you', your property and within your responsibility and ownership, and what is not. Boundaries are not usually explicitly taught, although there are some books that you can learn from, for example, Cloud and Townsend's *Boundaries* (1992), which is an excellent book from which I have learned many of the rules of boundaries, which I will explain below. The topic of boundaries is much larger than what I can fit in here, so I recommend that you get a copy of this book to learn more. I was stunned to discover how relevant this was to so much of my life, and how many of my problems relating to people actually are problems with boundaries. I need to know about boundaries to be aware of situations where someone is behaving in an unreasonable or abusive way to me, and in which I actually have a choice that I can make, and I need to use boundaries to say 'no' to people at appropriate times.

Boundaries is a massive topic which affects all relationships, including family, friends and work relationships – because in all human relationships there are choices to make, if you want something or if you do not. The relevance of boundaries to being safe with men is that sometimes you have to recognise when you have a right to say 'no' to something you do not want, to be able to say 'no', and to act on that. For example, if a man you are with wants to have sex with you, you have the choice and the right to say 'no' if you do not want to do this.

How do boundaries work?

If something is within your boundaries, then this means it is within your ownership and control. You can protect your boundaries by saying 'no' when other people ask for things that are within your boundaries but which you do not want to give to them.

You can choose to give things to others if they are within your boundaries, but this must be a free choice. Since what is within your boundaries is yours, the rule is that you only give it if you want to. Giving something that you do not want to give because you are scared of the consequences of not giving it, means that you do not have a boundary at all. For example, if I do overtime at work because I am afraid my boss will be angry if I do not, I am giving him something (my time) that is within my boundaries (I am not being paid for overtime) and that I do not want to give (my motivation is fear and not kindness). If I let someone kiss me when I do not want to, because I am afraid they will feel rejected if I do not, or that they will leave me if I do not, then I am not using any boundaries, because the person has got something from me that I did not freely want to give.

You can use boundaries to prevent things that are properly yours being taken from you against your will, and to give what is yours only when you genuinely want to. It is not selfish to have boundaries. Having boundaries does not mean that you will never give anything away. Instead, having boundaries means that you only give away what you truly want to.

The first crucial knowledge you need is what things are within your boundaries and are therefore your right to decide upon, and what things are not. Once you know this, the next thing to learn is how to say 'no' to people when they are asking you for something that you do not want to give, and to learn how to accept it when someone says 'no' to something that you have asked them for. By saying 'no', I mean not only literally and verbally saying 'no', but also any non-verbal form of communicating 'no' or refusing something.

What things are within your boundaries?

Some things within your boundaries (your control and ownership) include:

- *Your skin and your body*. Someone touching you is crossing into your space and into your boundaries. Your skin and your body belong to you. This means that you, and you alone, have the right to decide who can touch you and who cannot. This also means that you have the right to say 'no' if you do not want any particular person to touch you, to kiss you or to do any sexual act with you. This is your right to decide what happens to your body, not anyone else's. Equally, other people's skin belongs to them and they have the right to make decisions about their own body, not you. So if someone does not want you to touch them, you should respect their decision.

- *What you believe and think*. No-one else has the right to tell you what you should believe and what you should think, because these are your choices to make. Also, you do not have the right to tell anyone else what they should believe or think. I sometimes feel upset when someone I like very much does not think the same thing as me about moral issues that are important to me. But I have to remember that it is okay to disagree with people and I should not try to force them to agree with me (that would be me over-stepping into their boundaries – their right to decide what they believe and think). I also have to separate out in my mind liking/loving the person from not agreeing with them. It is possible to love someone but not share all of the same opinions on some important topics. Equally, if someone else does not agree with me, that does not mean that they do not like or respect me.

- *Your behaviour and your choices*. We cannot choose everything that happens to us, for example, I cannot control my boss's behaviour towards me. However, I can choose my response and my own behaviour towards him. I can choose not to stay in the same room as anyone who is behaving nastily or aggressively towards me. So, whilst you cannot stop anyone behaving as they want to, you can limit your exposure to their behaviour.

- *Your feelings*. You are responsible for your feelings and emotions. Other people are not responsible for your feelings and emotions. Of course, other people can have a positive or negative effect on us, and how they act towards us is not always fair. But it is your responsibility to recognise that you have a choice and to take the best action possible in the situation that you are in. The other person might have done something that you did not want, or not done something that you did want them to do. But, if you feel angry about this, you are responsible for your own anger and what to do about it. It is a good plan to avoid saying things such as 'He made me cross.' This sounds very accusatory to the other person. They might have done something that you did not like and you might have felt cross. But if you are feeling bad, this is your problem and not anyone else's. We cannot make other people responsible for our emotional well-being, because our emotional well-being is within our boundaries. Equally, we are not responsible for the emotional well-being of any other adult, because that is within their boundaries and not ours.

- *Your time.* You are in charge of your life and where you spend your time. Other people will want some of your time and will ask for this, but it is your decision whether you give it, and how much. For example, I like to talk to my friend on the telephone for a long time. But that is sometimes not convenient for her. When this happens, she will tell me that she only has ten minutes to give me, and after that, she will go. She decides how much of her time to allow me to share. It is my job to respect this, to not moan about it or try to manipulate her into giving me more time, even though I want this.

- *Your money.* You are in charge of your money. Again, other people will ask for this, and if you want to give money to them, you can, but you do not have to. Other people might put pressure on me to give money to them, but if I then do, I should not say 'They made me do it,' because although they have pressured me, I was the one who said 'yes'.

It is really important to know that you have control over all these things, and not other people. Often, when I find myself in a bad situation that I should have said 'no' to, it is because I simply have not been aware that I had a choice in the matter. I have not realised that other people are encroaching into my boundaries and I am allowing them to control aspects of my life that are really mine to control. I have kissed people who I did not want to kiss. I have done tasks at work that were stressful and not my job to do. I have allowed people to say things that hurt me, without defending myself or even telling them that I felt hurt by their words. We can only defend ourselves and stick up for ourselves when we are sure of what our rights and responsibilities actually are. So this list is very important to know and remember.

Saying 'no' to other people

Since boundaries define what is ours from what is not ours, and because we can only defend our boundaries by saying 'no', it is a crucial skill to be able to say 'no' to other people. I find this really hard. Many other people find this hard too. When it comes to things that are within our boundaries, it is important to be able to say things such as:

- 'No.'
- 'That is not fair.'
- 'I do not agree.'
- 'I will not.'
- 'Stop that.'
- 'That is wrong.'
- 'Sorry, I cannot help.'
- 'Sorry, I am not available.'
- 'Sorry, I will not do this because it is not in my job description.'
- 'Sorry, you cannot come in yet because you are too early.'
- 'I can only give you this much money.'
- 'I can only give you this much time.'
- 'I am not able to work overtime today.'
- 'No, you may not come in my bedroom/house.'
- 'I don't like it when you touch me like that.'
- 'Get your hands off me!'
- 'I will not have sex with you.'

It is also important to be able to say things such as, 'I felt hurt when you said such-and-such to me,' because often people hurt us unintentionally and if you do not say something about it, they will not learn how bad you felt and they might well do it again.

These are some of the words and phrases that you might need. However, as with most communication, how you say it is important, and this depends on the situation. In all situations, it is best to speak clearly and loud enough to sound firm and confident (pretend to be confident if you do not feel it). In many situations, a normal speaking loudness is fine. For example, if I am telling my boss that I will not do a piece of work, I want to say this to him nicely but firmly; I do not want to yell at him or whisper it.

However, if the other person is being aggressive, unreasonable, abusive or trying to intimidate you, you need a much louder voice. For example, if someone is touching you in an inappropriate way, you need to say 'Get your hands off me!' very loudly and forcefully. There are two reasons for this. First, the other person is more likely to take you seriously – saying it gently may have no effect. Second, although the words are addressed to the person touching you, there is a dual target for this communication – any other people nearby. That alerts other people to what is going on (who can perhaps come to your aid), and the fact that other people know will, it is hoped, scare the person off, because they do not want to get into trouble.

If you are not used to saying the sorts of things on this list (which I am not), a good idea is to role-play with someone else so that you can get some practice. Then, if you need to use them in real life, you will be more prepared and the phrases will be on the tip of your tongue. They look easy to say. But I find saying these things out loud to someone else extraordinarily difficult, even in role-play. So it might be worthwhile trying these out in role-play, even if you think you do not need to.

Why saying 'no' is hard: the Fear Factor

I find saying 'no' difficult because I am scared of the other person's reaction. I am mostly scared they might get angry or upset with me. I am scared of conflicts and disagreements.

It is certainly true that other people might get angry if you say 'no' to them. But, if the thing they wanted is within your boundaries and control to give or not to give, anyone being angry at you for refusing to give something that is yours, is being unreasonable and unfair on you. This is a really important point. I tend to assume if someone is upset with me, this is my fault, but very often this is not the case and they are upset because of their own issues and not because of me. This is a hard distinction for Aspies to make, because it is often really hard to be sure what the rights and wrongs of a social situation are. But if you are not sure about a situation, you can always ask one of your support network people whether someone's anger which is being aimed at you is justified or not.

If I continue to be too scared of conflicts to say 'no' to anything, I will always be giving away things that I do not wish to give away and I will feel sad, used and out of control. So, although I am trying to get myself a nice life by avoiding scary situations, I am not actually having a nice life.

Why saying 'no' might be harder for some people than for others

Some people find saying 'no' easy, and others, like me, find it hard. Whether we find saying 'no' easy or hard depends in part on our childhood experiences – what happened to you as a child when you did say 'no' to something and what you learned as a result. Lucky children learn that saying 'no' is a good thing, it protects them from what they do not want, that their 'no' is listened to and respected and that it is safe to say 'no' without risking a loss of love. These children are likely to grow up into adults who find it easy to say 'no'. Unluckier children learn that saying 'no' is a bad thing, that it gets them shouted at, that their 'no' is ignored, or that love is withdrawn from them when they say 'no'. These children are likely to grow up into adults who find it difficult to say 'no'.

I think as Aspies, in addition to the usual reasons that the general population would have, it is particularly hard for us to say 'no' because we tend to accumulate so much rejection, particularly in our early years. A lot of us become very eager to please other people in the hope that they will like us and not attack us; this is sometimes very much a matter of survival. I am not sure what I learned from my family. However, I definitely learned from school that I was at the bottom of the social hierarchy and that what everyone else wanted was more important than what I wanted – and indeed, the only chance I had to even be tolerated was to always go along with what others wanted. People-pleasing can become a deeply ingrained habit. Saying 'no' does not please other people, because everyone would ideally like their requests to be granted. If we have developed a deep belief from years of experience that we always have to comply with others in order to be accepted, liked or tolerated, then not complying by saying 'no' to something is likely to generate a great deal of anxiety.

Other reasons that saying 'no' is particularly difficult for me (and I am pretty sure other Aspies too) include that other people seem to have more common sense and more social knowledge than I do, and that I often do have different wishes and needs from other people (or at least I think I do, because I am comparing the genuine inside of me to society's superficial outside). This causes the problem that I feel unable to trust my own judgement. Since I often seem to be in the minority in holding any particular opinion, I tend to think that other people are always more right than me. I find myself thinking: 'I have to do this, even though I do not want to, because this is what seems to be society's norm and because it is expected of me to do it.' I now realise that this is faulty thinking because I always have a choice and it is actually okay for me to respect my own choices. By always deferring to what society expects, I am not loving myself, because I am disrespecting my own wishes in order to try to fit in.

Another Aspie-related reason that I find it hard to say 'no' is it often takes me a while to process information, to decide if someone's request is reasonable or not, and to work out how to respond. I often need to go away and think before I have the answer, but a response from me is often expected instantly. This makes it hard to give the right response. I might agree to something before having had the chance to reflect on what I really wanted and whether it is reasonable. I need to change my default response to 'no' in these circumstances.

If you say 'no' initially to a request when you are not actually sure, and then find later that you are able and willing to do it, you can normally change your mind later and say 'yes', and people will be delighted. However, if you say 'yes' initially to a request when you are not sure, but then find out later that this is a problem, you have a choice. You can either back out of it and change your 'yes' to a 'no', or you could follow through with your commitment. If you back out, you will look unreliable and people will be disappointed because you originally said 'yes'. If instead, you follow through with your commitment, part of you will be resentful because you really did not want to do it/give it, and you are now giving it reluctantly. Therefore, when in doubt, it is always best to say 'no' or 'let me think about that and get back to you' as a first response and then consider later, when you have enough time to make a proper decision. That way, you will gain a reputation for being reliable and honouring your promises, and you will be giving with a spirit of kindness and not resentment.

Because how we were raised as children and our general childhood experiences are a matter of luck, and because I am pretty sure that saying 'no' is much harder for Aspies than for most other people, do not worry if you, like me, are someone who finds it hard to say 'no'. This does not mean that you are an inferior person and it does not mean that you are weak. It simply means that you have been in a lot of situations in the past where saying 'no' was not safe for you. However, whether we find saying 'no' easy or hard, the good news is that this is a skill that we can all learn.

Even if saying 'no' was not safe in the past, when you were a little, powerless child, the situation has changed if you are now an adult. The same rules that were important and did previously keep you safe as a child (for example, 'I must always please other people'), may now be holding you back as an adult, hurting you and preventing you from looking after yourself and loving yourself. But the good news is, these are your rules, so you can change them if you want to.

Benefits of saying 'no' to others when we want to

I find that saying 'no' to other people takes a lot of courage and it is not something that I am used to at all. However, I have recently started doing this, and it can have some great payoffs. It is one of those things that is difficult and stressful to do in the short term, but it has the potential to be of great long-term benefit. For example, someone's behaviour was upsetting me and I was feeling very stressed being around them. I avoided saying anything about it for a long time, but after learning about boundaries, I eventually plucked up the courage to say something. I was very worried that the person would become tearful, upset and hurt. But in fact, the conversation went far better than I could have ever predicted. And the result was, I feel a lot safer around this person now, as I know I can protect myself by saying 'no' to behaviour that I do not like and by explaining that I feel stressed when they do or say particular things. A second example is that I have started refusing to take responsibility for other people's personal money at work. This was difficult to do at the time, and did cause some initial friction, but now, it has been agreed that this is not part of my job and I will not have to do it again. Therefore, my work stress has reduced.

So, the advantages of using boundaries include good long-term payoffs. The knowledge that we are able to use boundaries to protect ourselves (even simply by mentioning it when other people accidentally say things that hurt us) can give a big reduction in stress and anxiety. Basically, if you are brave enough to say what you want and what you do not want, what you like and what you do not like, and what you are willing to give and what you are not willing to give, you are much more likely to get your wishes granted and it definitely helps you feel more in control of your life.

Why you must learn to say 'no' in order to be safe with men

Protecting your boundaries by saying 'no' is not easy, but it is very important. Protecting your boundaries is particularly important when it comes to boyfriends and men in general. I have been bopping along in the world for most of my life without much of an ability to say 'no' to a lot of things and to a lot of people, and this is really dangerous. It means that men have been able to do with me, not quite whatever they wanted, but certainly more than I wanted them to. There is both good and evil in the world. Not being able to say 'no' means not being able to say 'no' to evil. Not being able to say 'no' is therefore a real disability and potentially dangerous; you are very vulnerable to abusive and controlling people. So, if you are like me in this way, it is time for both of us to be really brave, learn to say 'no' and to practise so that we can keep ourselves safe. For me, I have been able to say 'no' to some things and to some people, but there are certain things and certain people that I have not been able to say 'no' to at all. If you cannot say 'no' to anyone for anything, then dating and even simply being alone with a man is not going to be safe for you until you have learned how to do this. So, this is really important. We can both do this, because Aspies are very determined and very brave.

Learning how to say 'no'

No matter what our current skill level is (or level of fear), we can all learn proper boundaries and how to defend them by learning to say 'no'. Some people are easier to say 'no' to than others. For example, it is easier for me to say 'no' to one of my support network than it is to say 'no' to my boss. Some situations are easier to say 'no' to than others. For example, it is easier for me to tell someone that I do not want to see a particular film at the cinema, than it is for me to tell someone that I do not want to kiss them. So start small, with your safe people and really easy things to say 'no' to, and practise, so that you can eventually work up to the hard things with less safe people.

Another way to look at this is that if you cannot say 'no' to things you do not want, you are effectively lying about your wishes. I hate lying. This will motivate me to try hard to say 'no' in future.

Think about all the benefits of being able to say 'no' and the ways in which your life will be better in the long term. This can help motivate you to overcome the fear of saying 'no'.

One of my safe people has a very lovely way of saying 'no' to me. She often puts it in the form 'no, but…' For example, she might say, 'I do not have any time for you just now, but I can talk to you this evening.' Or she might say 'no' to the long chat that I was wanting, but 'yes' to the hug. Or she might say, 'I have to talk to someone else right now, but I can give you a lift home.' I find that the 'but…' really softens the blow of the 'no'. So, when you are learning to say 'no', you could use this technique too. However, there is no obligation to give a 'but' concession. Sometimes, the answer just has to be 'no' and you are not obliged to offer anything else instead.

Hearing 'no' from other people

Of course, we should always treat others the way we wish to be treated ourselves. We would like other people to respect our boundaries and respect it when we say 'no' to them. Therefore, we must also respect other people's boundaries, and respect it when other people say 'no' to our request for something that is within their boundaries, their control and their ownership.

Respecting other people's boundaries means being able to hear 'no' from them regarding something that you wanted from them but did not have a right to have, without behaving in a cross and angry way towards them, seeking revenge or seeking to control them and force them to change their mind and give you what you wanted (either manipulatively or aggressively). An example of aggressive behaviour is shouting or threatening someone to try to force them to change their mind. An example of manipulative behaviour is trying to make someone feel guilty so that they will give you what you want – for example by saying, 'If you truly loved me, you would spend the weekend with me,' or 'I am just so busy, and I know that you will not mind babysitting for me.'

As well as avoiding aggressive and manipulative behaviours yourself, watch out for being on the receiving end of these from others when you say 'no' to them. People who are not able to respect other people's boundaries are not going to be well liked by others and may do quite a lot of damage to other people. You may know people like this. Do not be like them.

When I ask for something from someone else, it is never nice for me to hear 'no' because I am hoping for a 'yes' and I feel disappointed not to get what I want. This is true for everyone; no-one actually likes hearing a 'no' from anyone else. However, mature people are able to deal with receiving a 'no' from someone else without launching nasty behaviour on them (aggressively or manipulatively), in an attempt to change their 'no' into a 'yes'. The mature response is to take it with good grace – for example, smile, say, 'Okay, that is fine,' and respect their right to say 'no'. This is an act of love and kindness towards them. Accepting someone's 'no' means that you are truly accepting the whole person and you are helping them protect the things that rightfully belong to them. If you love someone, you have to value and respect their 'no' as much as their 'yes', in the same way that we would like others to respect it when we say 'no' to their requests for things that belong to us. It is unfair only to be nice to someone when they are prepared to give you what you want.

Feeling hurt or pain when someone says 'no' to you

Two different reasons for feeling hurt are:

1. someone refusing to give you something from within their boundaries

2. someone taking something from you that was rightfully yours.

Although you may feel disappointed or even hurt when you request something that is within someone else's boundaries to give (for example, their time, help or money) and you receive a 'no', it is really important to remember that they have not actually acted badly towards you by saying 'no', because the thing they did not give you was always theirs and never yours.

This is very different from someone stealing from you something that originally was yours. For example, if a thief steals your wallet, your anger and upset is entirely justified because they have taken something that properly belonged to you.

To me, both these situations feel similar because they both generate hurt, so I find it helpful to think about boundaries to work out which type of situation it is, because only then can I work out if the person has behaved fairly to me or not. The first situation can cause me to feel sad, hurt, upset and angry. But the other person has not done anything wrong to me, so I need to be careful to recognise this and not react in any kind of unpleasant way towards them.

Difficulties with hearing 'no' from others

Where some people go wrong is becoming aggressive, intimidating or controlling in response to hearing 'no' from others.

Where I personally go wrong the most is that I have a tendency to want other people to be responsible for my emotional well-being. I desperately want other people to rescue me from situations that I find difficult. I was surprised to find that these are both boundary violations. It is rather ironic: I take responsibility for other people's feelings (for example, I worry about them becoming angry) when I should not, because that is within their boundaries and not mine; and then I fail to take responsibility for my own feelings! I have it exactly the wrong way round, which I understand is also pretty common.

I have made mistakes in the past by assuming that the following situations might make my own emotional well-being someone else's responsibility instead of my own:

- when I am in a huge amount of pain
- when I feel that my pain was caused by an unfair situation
- when I feel unable to cope with my pain
- because the other person loves me
- because I have become used to receiving help when I ask for it.

But there is nothing in the rules of boundaries that says the amount of pain, the seriousness of the situation or the fairness of the situation changes the fact that my emotional well-being is within my boundaries and is no-one else's responsibility.

Equally, my own lack of competence does not make my emotional well-being someone else's problem. In broader terms, anyone's argument along the lines, 'Because I am so pathetic at this (thing in their own boundaries, for example, making decisions, controlling their emotions, doing a particular work task, etc.), therefore you must either do it for me or help me with it,' is wrong. Lack of competence at anything falling within someone's boundaries still does not make this anyone else's responsibility. Watch out in case you receive this kind of argument from other people – and make sure that you recognise that it is wrong.

Just because someone has been very kind and has helped me a lot in the past, there is no rule that they will *always* help me whenever I happen to want it or need it. When I thought about this properly, this is ridiculous. They do not owe me their help. It might not be convenient for them.

I have wrongly assumed that if someone loves me, that makes them obliged to help me whenever I really need it, and if they say 'no', that means they cannot really love me and that they have abandoned me. But the boundaries rules apply to all people. Even people who love me still always retain their right to protect their own boundaries by saying 'no' to me, and if I truly love them back, I must respect this. After some thought (and prompting by a friend), I worked out that the real rules are:

- People who I love do not have to do what I want them to.

- If someone does not do what I want them to, that does not mean that they do not love me.

Why I like being 'rescued' by others

Although I really do not want to admit this, because I know it is wrong and because I feel scared and guilty about it, I can easily get overly dependent on a small number of people who help me understand the world and who are able to rescue me from my difficult emotional situations by calming me down and stabilising my emotions. I then find I would rather be rescued by them from a difficult emotional situation than solve it myself. I want them to be responsible for my emotional well-being. In my head, this is really simple and logical. If I am rescued, my problem is solved quickly and efficiently and I feel loved, understood and protected. I feel amazing. But solving it myself is harder, more time-consuming and less efficient. Maintaining my own emotional well-being is definitely an area of weakness for me and I often do not believe that I can do it and, even if it works, *I do not get the benefits of feeling loved, understood and protected, which is what I am really seeking above all else.*

Why over-dependence is a bad thing

So, in view of the advantages of feeling loved and protected, why would I ever want to change? Actually, there are lots of good reasons:

- I am putting an unreasonable pressure on other people.
- The boundaries rules say this is not okay and it is a boundary violation, and I can see these rules are fair, so I want to follow them.
- I would be completely freaked out if someone else made me responsible for their emotional well-being – partly because I know I could not do it, and partly because it is unfair. So, if I would not like to receive this behaviour from others, I must not do it to others.
- I am making myself dependent, which is a child state and not an adult state.

- I am not learning the skill of taking care of my own emotional well-being.

- Being dependent is taking up a lot of my emotional energy, which could be better spent on other things.

- All humans are fallible, will let you down sometimes, only have a finite capacity to give, and, quite rightly, have the right to refuse to give. When this happens, if I am still a skill-free zone, I will not be able to help myself.

- I feel much more pain than is normal whenever someone that I really need says 'no' to me, and I find this pain is actually increasing over time.

- Being overly dependent on someone will probably make them feel something between uncomfortable and freaked out; they will have to say 'no' to me to keep me at a distance, and I am going to feel very hurt and rejected.

- If I carry on being overly dependent, I will drive away the people I need the most, and the pain, grief and the loss that I am so much wanting to avoid is going to happen to me anyway.

- Unless I change, I will always be drawn to repeat this pattern in the future.

- If I become overly dependent on someone (a man or a woman), I am going to find it almost impossible to say 'no' to them for anything. I am not going to be safe with anyone who I cannot say 'no' to.

Where I have been going wrong is trying to get from other people the unconditional love and approval that is not already lodged deeply within myself. This does not work. I have been trying to fill a deep emptiness in me with things from other people, and that appears to work over the short term, and to some extent, but ultimately, it is like trying to fill a bucket with a hole in. However much love other people put in is never enough, and I just want more and more and more, but I am never satisfied and the emptiness is never filled.

I will work on my ability to love and care for myself and to find other ways of meeting my needs. I will work on my own weaknesses and learn new skills. I hope, in time, I will become better at protecting myself by using good boundaries with others and in this way, I will become more loving towards myself, my relationships will go more successfully, and I will therefore have less of a need for a deep dependence on others for my own protection, safety and well-being.

Aspies often have difficulty with things that are not black and white, because we are, at heart, very simple people. But dependence is one of these annoying grey areas, because we do all need each other (which is what your support network is all about), so dependence to some extent is not bad. Also, the other extreme of acting like, or convincing yourself, that you do not need anyone at all is actually bad. The scale of dependence is like a line with total independence at one end of the scale (0), and over-dependence at the other end (100), with the best place being somewhere in the middle (50). I learned very easily that being dependent on others to some extent, and not being completely isolated, has wonderful benefits. So, in true Aspie fashion, I do it more and more. But I am learning in a very hard way that this can easily go too far into over-dependence. So, how on earth can anyone know how much dependence is too much? Well, I would measure it by the amount of pain that you feel when someone says 'no' to you for something. Some level of discomfort is normal, because no-one likes getting their requests denied. But if the pain is excessive, you may be too dependent.

CHAPTER 3

Useful Rules

Rules can be formed by your past experiences. Some rules are conscious – you are aware that you have them. Other rules are subconscious – you may not be aware of them.

Subconscious rules are tricky because it is hard to know what they are and they are buried quite deep down in the brain. The first challenge is becoming aware of them. Since they are not conscious, you have to sneak up on them. I do this by paying attention to my initial reaction to what other people say, and to any feeling of surprise that I have by my own thoughts. My subconscious response is my initial, gut reaction to something, before I have had time to think. For example, I was feeling anxious about going back to work after a period of absence, because my colleagues might ask me questions about things that had happened at work whilst I was away and I might not know the answers. My counsellor asked what that would mean about me if I did not know the answer. My initial reaction was that if I did not know the answer, that meant I was stupid. My more conscious response, a few seconds later, was that no-one could know everything that had happened at work in their absence and that my initial reaction was illogical. My subconscious and conscious responses were so different that I wondered if I had imagined the very fleeting subconscious response.

So, I have a subconscious belief/fear that I am stupid and a subconscious rule that if I do not know all the answers, I must be stupid. My conscious brain knows this belief and this rule are a load of rubbish, but they are still there in my subconscious. I am only aware of them because I managed to catch hold of my very instant reaction to the question. Therefore, it is possible to believe two contradictory things at the same time, on different levels, and many people do. Bizarre, but true.

These subconscious rules are like secret programming in your brain – they are always operating and having an effect. When I feel anxious, it is usually because I have a bad rule operating at the subconscious level and I am failing to keep my rule. The rule may be bad because it is impossible to keep, or because it is overly demanding (for example, 'I must always do everything that other people ask of me'). Breaking my rule means danger, therefore I feel anxious.

Rules can also be formed by you deciding to adopt a new rule and making a big effort to change your thinking. You can do this by:

- Writing the new rule down and reading it frequently.

- Saying the new rule out loud to yourself. By reading it or hearing yourself say it, the new rule enters your brain as a new input from outside.

- Asking other people to help by affirming the new rule to you. This works well for me because I tend to believe what other people say.

- Calling the new rule to mind in an appropriate situation. For example, I go to work by train and one of my old rules was, 'I must never miss a train.' This was a bad rule because it was causing a lot of panic and rushing. Now, when I feel myself starting to worry and rush for a train, I can think instead of my new rule: 'It is okay if I miss this train; I can get the next one.'

A big effort to change your thinking is needed for any of your rules which live at the subconscious level. I can change my conscious thinking in five seconds, just by deciding to, if someone tells me a new rule and I realise this rule is a good one. But changing deep, subconscious thinking takes longer. The first step to changing any bad, subconscious rules you may have is to make them conscious by becoming aware of what they are. The second step is to know what some good, alternative rules are.

Here are some rules which might help with relationships. I needed to work these out, because the opposites of these rules were actually in my head. I am still in the process of embedding some of these new rules into my brain.

Rule 1: I do not have to be perfect. It is okay to make mistakes

Many Aspie girls try to be perfect. This is what I tend to do. I thought for years that this was a good thing, because this quality in me was often praised and encouraged by others. It is true that aiming for perfection has some good aspects to it. For example, because I am trying to be perfect, I am careful and accurate with my work.

However, trying to be perfect also has a bad side. It causes me lots of stress and anxiety and means that I often put unnecessary pressure on myself. Trying to be perfect makes me very afraid of making mistakes, so I become afraid of trying new things. But if I do not try new things, I do not get new experiences and I cannot learn, change or grow. Trying to be perfect means that I feel very upset with myself when I make mistakes and I become critical towards myself. Being critical with myself is the opposite of loving myself, and it is very important to love myself.

Therefore, on the whole, trying to be perfect is a bad thing. That is not to say that I should not try at all. But if things do not work out quite as I had intended, I can choose not to beat myself up.

Therefore, the new rule is that I do not have to be perfect. It is okay to make mistakes. Mistakes are valuable learning opportunities and provide the chance to grow and mature.

Rule 2: I am precious and I have great worth. I deserve good people in my life. I will not give myself away to just anyone who will have me

If you have experienced a lot of rejection in your life, the natural rule formed by these experiences is that you have very little worth. This is certainly a rule that I had.

If you believe that you have little worth, you are more likely to accept people who treat you badly. You might accept men treating you badly and abusing you. You might pick the wrong sort of man if you believe that no-one decent would ever want you. You might accept someone who you do not love as your boyfriend, simply because they will have you, even if you are not particularly interested in them. A rule that says that you are not worth much is a bad rule.

Recently, some people have started telling me that I am precious. This was a bit of a revelation! I am precious and valuable because of my soul, not because of anything I have achieved. I am precious and valuable because of all the good parts of me, even though there are some bad parts too. We are all a mixture of good and bad.

Therefore, the new rule is that I am precious and I have great worth. I deserve good people in my life. I will not give myself away to just anyone who will have me.

Rule 3: It is okay to develop at my own pace

A lot of the mistakes I have made with men have been due to feeling a huge pressure from society to have a boyfriend and to have romantic relationships. Usually, I have been trying to do this because I thought I should, at times when my peer group was doing it, but I have not felt ready.

I have a theory that Aspies live on a different timescale to other people. I remember at age 10, my classmates all mentally changing a great deal (into adolescents), and me staying the same and still feeling like a child. Actually, I still feel much more like a child now than an adult. Although I have learned to do adult things and live in an adult world, it does not feel as if 'adult' is what I am. I am now 34 but I am often mistaken for a teenager.

I had an old rule that I must keep up with other people. I must achieve everything my sister does. I should have a boyfriend by such-and-such an age. I should be married by such-and-such an age. I should have children by such-and-such an age. I should have a high-flying career. I should at least feel like an adult. This was a bad rule. It made me feel bad and guilty, slow and stupid. It encouraged me to do things that I did not feel ready for. This was not a recipe for success. Trying relationships before I was ready was always unlikely to work, however much I wanted it to. So, this rule made me feel bad and did not get me what I wanted.

One of the difficulties is that people like me tend to get called 'emotionally immature' by non-spectrum people, which is pretty insulting and strengthens the old and very bad rule that we must keep up with other people.

The result of all of this was that I felt very ashamed of who I was. This actually became much more of a problem when I got braver and started to show people who I was. Whilst I was hiding, I was doing a fair impression of normal and I did not feel particularly different or ashamed. But when I started reacting more spontaneously, acting out of my heart rather than how I thought I should, it became much more obvious that who I was, was rather different. For example, I used to go to night clubs and look fairly normal even if I did not enjoy it. Now, I go into a playground with my friends' children and go down the slides with the five-year-olds. At a party, you are more likely to find me in shorts and T-shirt on a trampoline with the children, than standing around in a posh dress with the women. I am much happier doing what comes naturally to me to do, but I am suddenly very aware of sticking out. I love it, but I found this new feeling of shame, too. I thought I was emotionally immature (someone had called me that) and that this was a moral character failing because I should be more 'grown up'. Feeling ashamed of who I was prevented me from accepting myself.

My safe person helped me with this when she said that I have always felt like an ugly duckling but actually I am a swan. I was listening very seriously until she followed it up with: 'But there is one thing you have to realise – you will never be a duck!' and then I fell about laughing.

I think this means that even the best possible and most mature version of me is never going to be or look quite the same as a non-spectrum woman, but what I am is very beautiful nonetheless. I am not a gone-wrong or morally defective version of normal – which is what 'emotionally immature' implies. I am on a different developmental track; it had a different beginning, it has a different middle, it will have a different end and it was never meant to be the non-spectrum track. So, comparisons with non-spectrum people's development are wrong (but so tempting and difficult to avoid, because I spend most of my time in a non-spectrum environment).

We do grow up and develop when we are given the right people and the right circumstances. But we are very sensitive and things like rejection, being misunderstood, our needs not being met, or being criticised or judged can hurt us very deeply and cause us to build walls around our hearts for our own protection. These walls do protect us but they keep other people out and keep us from learning things like trust, vulnerability and being connected to others, which are skills everyone needs before they can learn that they are lovable and acceptable. Also, even if the right support is there, we just may not be ready to learn the things that other people are ready for at the same chronological age.

The result is, we may have to learn some things in adulthood that other people learn as children, and we may need the same unconditional love, gentleness, acceptance and learning environment that a child would need. This may be quite hard to find because for most other people, this need of ours would be very unexpected. Whether and when we learn and grow is not any moral failure on our part, but is dependent on us being in the right environment. A seed cannot grow if no-one plants or waters it. We cannot grow ourselves up or control this process. What we can do is try our best to find the people we need and then have the courage to trust them and make ourselves vulnerable to them by taking down our own heart defences, being very honest and showing them who we are. I had no idea that I was doing any of this, but I seem to have done it by accident and it was definitely the right path. This has to be our choice; no-one can break down our defences for us, and the more forceful the approach, the more defences we will fling up. The best that other people can do is offer gentleness, acceptance, help, compassion and comfort, without any criticism, judgement or expectation. Then it is our choice to respond or not.

I now think some of the things I was worrying about were not causes for alarm. Actually, slides and trampolines *are* fun and I think the non-spectrum adult world is rather missing out – some of them are just too afraid to do these fun things in case they do not look normal. The biggest fear that most non-spectrum people have is what other people will think. This is not generally our biggest fear, so it is easier for us to choose to be different – this is an advantage of being an Aspie.

It is better to re-frame 'emotionally immature' more positively as 'young at heart'. There is nothing wrong or bad about being young at heart. In fact, being young at heart has the following advantages:

- Children can relate to me very easily and I can relate to them easily too.

- I am not cynical or jaded.

- I am a simple person.

- I have simple joys.
- I am always learning and developing.
- There are parts of me that are pure and unspoiled because there are certain vices and bad habits that I have not developed.
- I have not conformed enough to the world to lose some of my values.
- I can do things that most other adults would be too self-conscious to do.
- I have an openness that other adults do not have.
- I have an innocence that other adults do not have.
- Other people can enjoy that I am different to them.
- Having to live in the adult world and fend for myself has meant that I have had to develop huge amounts of courage.
- Nice people sense my vulnerability and have an instinct to love and protect me.

Therefore, the new rule is that it is okay to develop at my own pace.

Rule 4: It is okay to be different. It is okay to be myself

I had an old rule that it is not okay to be different. If anyone has experienced a lot of rejection because they are different, this is a natural rule to have. I only realised that I had this rule, and that I believed it very strongly indeed, when someone first told me that it *is* okay to be different. The amount of surprise I felt told me that, deep down, I did not believe this.

The consequences of having this old rule were that I spent a lot of energy trying to conform, and to hide who I really was from other people. I did not feel close to anyone because I never showed them who I was. I also felt like I was wrong and bad for being different. Hiding my difference just made me more sure that I was wrong and bad – otherwise why would I be hiding it? Hiding my difference meant that other people could not see who I really was, or affirm and love who I was. I did not enjoy the effects of this rule.

The new rule is that it is okay to be different. You do not have to conform to what society says is the right thing to be or to do. You can just be yourself. Therefore, if you do not want to have a boyfriend, you do not have to have one. It is okay to be single. If you do not want a boyfriend yet, that is okay too, and you can always change your mind in the future.

It takes a tremendous amount of courage for Aspies to stop hiding, and you have to make yourself vulnerable to do this, so it is important to have the right support network around you. Following the new rule has the advantages that people can truly know me and love me, and that I do not have to feel pressured into 'pretending to be normal' or conforming to things that are wrong for me.

I am discovering that my differences of being more open, more innocent, simpler, more honest, more gentle, less self-conscious and more childlike than most other adults can sometimes be real advantages in social interaction. These can be disarming and can get past other people's defences. After reading so much about Aspies being defined as having an impairment in social interaction, it is like an earthquake happening in my heart to realise the truth: that being an Aspie gives me some advantages in social interaction, too.

Therefore, the new rule is that it is okay to be different.

Rule 5: You cannot control other people or change them. Therefore you cannot control your dating life or other relationships

You cannot control or change other people. You can only control and change yourself.

Relationships involve two people, not just you. Therefore, you cannot force a relationship to happen. You can create circumstances in which you are more likely to meet a suitable partner, but you cannot make it happen and it is stressful to try.

It is often said that Aspies do not like change. But actually, non-spectrum people often do not like change either. And changing oneself in any way, for example, maturing, developing and creating new ways of thinking and behaving, is very difficult for everyone, no matter who they are. Many people die each year from smoking-related illnesses, alcohol or obesity because they choose not to change the bad habits that are killing them. Amazing as it seems, humans actually find change so difficult that many people die because they choose not to change.

Therefore, if someone has a personal quality or habit that you do not like, you should not expect them to change if you go out with them or if you marry them. Only go out with them or marry them if you already accept all of who they presently are. What you do have power to do is to change yourself, and you can learn to set boundaries with people whose behaviour is having a bad effect on you.

Therefore, the rule is that you cannot control other people or change them.

Rule 6: It is okay to trust. It is okay to trust myself

I found out that I had a rule against trusting when my friend said that it is okay to trust. Immediately, I had a very loud thought that said, 'No, it's not.' I felt surprised that I have this rule.

If you have been let down many times in the past by other people, if your trust has frequently been abused, it is natural to have a rule that it is not okay to trust anybody.

The rule of not trusting people has the advantage that it protects you from certain types of harm and hurt. If everyone you know hurts you or behaves horribly, it is a good idea not to trust them.

However, the world is full of all sorts of people. Having a blanket rule about not trusting anyone means that you cannot be vulnerable to anyone, you cannot be truly known or loved (because you cannot trust people enough to show them who you really are) and you miss opportunities to discover people who really are trustworthy and who will honour your trust. If you do not trust, you miss out on closeness. Romantic relationships are not worth much if there is no mutual trust. If you do not trust, you miss out on the good things that can result if the trust is honoured. For example, if I decide never to get married because I cannot trust any men, then I lose out on the potential love, comfort and intimacy of being married. Not trusting anyone keeps you isolated from the good, as well as from the bad. Not trusting anyone is to have boundaries that always stay closed, to everyone.

Therefore, the new rule is that it is okay to trust. This does not mean that it is okay to trust everyone, without discrimination.

Trusting anyone involves making yourself vulnerable. If mostly, you know nice people, what happens is that most people will honour your trust, and a few people will not. You can expect a few bad experiences to happen. However, when these bad experiences do happen, what to learn is not to trust these specific people again, without a very good reason. Do not impose a blanket ban on trusting anyone, ever again.

I also have a very hard time trusting myself, because I seem to get things wrong so often and because other people seem to be right much more often than me. However, not trusting myself in certain situations is spilling over into not trusting myself even in situations where I know that I am competent and in which I have always succeeded in the past. This is causing panic attacks over the simplest things, such as doing the food shopping, which I never had before.

Therefore, the new rule is that it is okay to trust. I can also choose to trust myself, which is a very simple attitude adjustment and which is already lessening the panic attacks.

Rule 7: Obsessions with people are not allowed

Aspies' interests tend to be narrow and deep, in contrast to non-spectrum people's interests, which tend to be broad and shallow. This means that we are not interested in a huge number of things, but if we are interested in something, we are deeply interested and this interest can become an obsession. Obsessions can be activities, things and facts. Some of my obsessions include ice-skating, cats and autism.

People can also be the subject of an obsession. In just the same way that I have a narrow, deep interest in autism, I can have a narrow, deep interest in certain people.

I heard Rudy Simone (an Aspie) give a talk recently, and she said the rule is that obsessions with things are fine but obsessions with people are not. There are disadvantages of having an obsession with a person. If you become obsessed with someone who is not a nice person, they could treat you badly and you might put up with it because you like them so much and just want to be around them. Even if you become obsessed with a nice person, they might feel suffocated. Non-spectrum people tend to need a large number of people in their lives – probably more than we do – and they have to juggle their time between all of them. If you are too clingy to one person, they will eventually decide to fend you off, and that will really hurt. Even if you are married to the person you are obsessed with, your husband will still need his own space and time for his own friends and interests. In my experience, obsessions with people start off feeling great but are ultimately painful and I find myself losing some of my freedom and independence.

Rudy Simone also said that we Aspies often do not see the need for more than one friend, and I think she is totally right. However, this has the big disadvantage that all your eggs are in one basket. If we only have one friend, we become very vulnerable to their saying 'no' to us and it hurts a lot. But other people have their own lives to lead and no-one can be always available to us whenever we need them. It is much safer to have a network of friends and relationships that we can rely on in times of need. If one person is not available, we can try someone else.

But obsessions are so inherently pleasurable (which is why they are obsessions) that how do you stop yourself having one? This was not at all obvious to me. I think this is a really, really hard thing to do. It hurts me intensely and is one of the most painful things I know. I think some pain is probably inevitable because giving up an obsession is a loss, and losses hurt. The feeling that accompanies this hurt is called grief. When I experience grief, I have frequent periods of crying and of feeling a wide range of negative emotions such as anger, guilt, shame, fear and sadness. This is normal. It feels like the pain will never end and that it will not be possible to endure. But it will eventually end and it can be endured.

I think the best way to deal with grief is:

1. Cry and express your sadness but limit how much time you do this each day and do not neglect any self-care aspects, socialising or other things you need to do to carry on functioning. Continue to love yourself. Give yourself a distraction and a treat after your 'crying time' is up.

2. Tell someone else how you are feeling, so that they can comfort you and you are not all alone with your pain.

3. Do not be ashamed. Having obsessions is part of being an Aspie, and it is up to us to learn how to handle them in the best possible way. You are not a bad person for having an obsession.

4. Stop longing for what you have lost. If possible, it might be a good idea to stop seeing the person completely for as long as it takes for your emotions to stabilise and for the obsession to disappear.

5. Be grateful for all of the good things the relationship with that person has given you; for example, joy, encouragement, wisdom and personal growth. These are gifts that stay with you even if the person is not there.

6. Focus your energies in another direction. Instead of thinking, 'I must stop this obsession with so-and-so', which does not work at all, will make you feel guilty and hurt very badly (by trying to stop something you are constantly reminded of what it is that you are trying to stop, which makes stopping it practically impossible), try thinking, 'I can concentrate more on my relationships with a wide range of other people.'

Different people experience grief in different ways and for different lengths of time. I have found that doing these six things helps me to move on from my grief, and that not doing them prolongs the grief.

Therefore, the new rule is that obsessions with people are not allowed. I can also use my strengths of obedience and rule-following to help me obey this rule. If I think of this as a rule, I am more likely to follow it.

Rule 8: I deserve to be loved

A belief that you do not deserve to be loved by others is probably the worst thing about having low self-esteem.

If you do not believe that you deserve love or that you deserve good things, it starts to become a self-fulfilling prophecy. I am not sure exactly how this happens, but I guess that when you feel miserable about yourself, your body language and face reflect how you feel and that looks very unattractive to other people. It makes you talk in a gloomy, negative way and then you are not as fun to be around (think Eeyore from Winnie-the-Pooh). It makes you look out for the negatives (because they are what you are expecting) and ignore the positives. Essentially, you give off 'bad vibes' which are not attractive to the positive people who you want and need in your life. However, bad, manipulative people can see them and you become a magnet to them instead, because these self-beliefs make you isolated and vulnerable and bad people may wish to exploit this. Also, good but negative people who also do not believe they deserve to be loved will sense a sameness with you and be attracted to you, and then you can be both giving out and receiving negativity from each other.

I used to believe that I did not deserve to be loved. I do not believe this anymore. I only knew I had this belief when someone asked me if I thought that I deserved to be loved, and my quick, unthinking response was a very strong 'no'. I wrote this in my diary. Four years later, I re-read my diary and realised this was no longer true, to my great surprise.

I did not consciously change this belief or do anything myself which caused it to change, except seek out nice people and trust them. The only thing that happened in that four years was that I had some people be very nice to me and very accepting of me, patiently and consistently, over this period of time. This belief is very closely tied to how you are treated by other people. The brain seems to take people's treatment of you as a measure of what you deserve.

Therefore, what you need is some other people who will wrap you up in their arms, who will comfort you when you cry, who will love and not reject even the worst parts of you (we are all a mixture of good and bad), who will know and accept you for who you really are, and who will tell you, very clearly, literally and explicitly that you are precious, that you are special, that you have great worth, that you are deserving, that you are lovable, and who identify and tell you about all your good qualities. All you have to do is find the right people, or the right person, and then trust them. When other people treat you as if you are lovable, you start to believe that you deserve it.

Therefore, the new rule is that I deserve to be loved.

Rule 9: I am not stupid

As I explained at the start of this chapter, I have a subconscious belief that I am stupid. Although I know theoretically that I am intelligent (I have enough exam results and other achievements to prove that), I spend a lot of my life feeling really stupid – for example, when people call me naive, when someone manages to lie to me or take advantage of me, when people get angry at me for something that I did not mean, when I have tried to communicate about something important and it does not work, or when I manage to make yet another mistake about something that would have been obvious to other people. I understand that feeling stupid is a common Aspie experience.

The last time I was talking about a situation in which I had been taken advantage of, I confided to my safe person that I felt really stupid, and she said that I was not stupid, but I had just been blind-sided on the face of my disability. That made me feel a lot better and I think this is a good way to look at it.

Therefore, the new rule is that I am not stupid. Being an Aspie means that some things are very much harder for me to work out than they would be for other people. This does not mean that I am stupid. I have plenty of other evidence that I am not stupid. The belief that I am stupid is a very deep belief that must have started from when I was very young and has been reinforced a lot since, so I am going to ask other people to keep affirming to me that I am not stupid, to help me believe it.

Rule 10: I am not selfish

Rudy Simone said that Aspie girls are often labelled as self-absorbed. I have been called selfish by someone close to me, and although this was many years ago, this has really stuck in my heart. As with so many words from other people, I accepted the label of being selfish at a deep, literal level, without questioning it. Once in your head, this is a difficult label to get out of it. Other people have now said I am not selfish, but I have not quite managed to believe this yet.

Selfishness is a general human quality and everyone can behave selfishly at one time or another. But I do think it is wrong to label people as selfish – it is certainly incredibly damaging. We all have a choice with our words, whether we use them to bless or to curse, to heal or to damage. My counsellor says that what happened to me was that at a certain time in the past, someone perceived my behaviour in a particular situation to be selfish, and that it is up to me if I choose to take this person's frame of reference forward.

I think Aspies are particularly at risk of getting labelled as selfish, in error, by others. We do not automatically know what other people are thinking and feeling. So, we can sometimes act without regard to other people's feelings. But this might be because we do not know what these feelings are; not because we do know and we are choosing to ignore them. Out of two options, we might simply pick what we prefer, without regard to any other consideration. But it is not possible to have regard to other people's feelings when we do not know what they are. So, we can get mistakenly labelled as selfish for something which is not our fault at all. One thing I certainly know about me and my Aspie friends (and probably most Aspies in the world) is that we never intend to cause any harm. Another reason is that sometimes doing things that non-spectrum people expect us to do (for example, attend important social events) might have a big cost to us, which is hidden from them, and we might therefore choose not to do them. For example, if your friend had a birthday party, and you chose not to go because you felt really anxious about it, other people who do not understand might think your decision was selfish.

There is also the possibility for human error. In my case, the person was trying to force me to do something that I did not want to do, and which was a choice that was within my boundaries to make. When I did not agree, I was called selfish. The lesson from this is that other people (even authority figures) are not always right.

A disadvantage of believing and fearing that I am selfish is that I am always looking out for evidence that supports this belief and I sometimes find myself construing my behaviour as selfish when it actually is not (see example in rule 11, in which I mistakenly thought I was selfish for blessing myself). Another disadvantage is that it is causing me to hate myself instead of love myself.

Therefore, the new rule is that I am not selfish. I might do some things that are selfish and other things that are not, on particular occasions. But selfishness is a description of a behaviour at a particular time and is no longer a label that I accept for myself as a person.

Rule 11: It is okay to love myself.
It is important to love myself.
It is not selfish to love myself

It has always seemed to me wrong to love myself. This is a low self-esteem thing. I received a blessing for my birthday, which I framed and put on my wall. It starts: 'The Lord bless you and keep you.' I was trying to get into the habit of speaking compassionately to myself and I said to myself: 'The Lord bless me and keep me.' I realised I had got the words wrong and I immediately felt guilty and selfish for blessing myself – which caused a panic attack.

My safe person told me it is important to love myself. 'Okay,' I thought, 'but how do I do that?' I have been struggling with this for ages, which has been very frustrating. Either I am just not getting it, people are not being clear enough for me, or maybe the ways that other people use are just not the right ways for me. I suspect a combination of these. 'Love yourself' is actually just a vague instruction to achieve a certain goal – but that is not nearly clear enough for me; I need precise instructions. Anyway, I think I am starting to get it now. Here are the steps I recommend:

1. Understand why loving yourself is a good thing to do and get any thoughts out of your head that it is wrong or selfish

Advantages of loving yourself include that you feel good about yourself and being you, you can focus on getting your needs met, you speak to yourself in a kind way, and you take better care of yourself.

Disadvantages of not loving yourself include low self-esteem, neglecting to take care of your needs in favour of everyone else's and accepting ill-treatment from others because you believe that you do not deserve anything better.

Also, if you are an adult, you are primarily the person whose job it is to love and take of yourself; it is no-one else's job. This is a very inconvenient truth for me, because I would really like other people to take care of me, but it is still the truth and we must all work with the world as it is, not how we would like it to be. Other people look after themselves. So if you do not look after yourself, what happens is that your needs get neglected. Also, if you do not love yourself, other people will have a hard time loving you, because you are working against them. Their love for you might not make sense with your self-image, so you might reject it even if you want to accept it, or never even notice it in the first place.

In the Bible, it is said that Jesus told us to love our neighbour as ourselves. This presupposes that we do love ourselves; it is so strongly assumed that the author did not even write it explicitly. Otherwise, the sentence would mean that we should not love ourselves or our neighbour. Whatever you believe or do not believe, the Bible is not generally thought to be a book which encourages selfishness.

I have also heard it said a lot that in order to be able to properly love someone else, you have to love yourself first. If you are a miserable, worn-out dish rag, ill and drained of energy because you are not loving yourself or taking care of yourself, you are not going to able to help others, in any way. It is not selfish to love others. Therefore, if we need to love ourselves first in order to be able to love others, it is not selfish to love ourselves.

In summary, good things happen when you love yourself and bad things happen when you do not. Therefore, the new rule is that it is okay to love myself, it is important to love myself and it is not selfish to love myself. I can bless myself and be good to myself and that does not mean that I am selfish. Hence, I do not need to feel guilty or wrong for loving myself.

2. Recognise your needs and communicate them

Love is an action, not just a feeling.

Your body has needs. Some of these needs are to get enough food and to get enough rest. I tend to forget about my body and act as if I am just a floating head, but this is a very bad idea. A body that is hungry and exhausted is not going to feel loved by you. To love yourself and to feel loved, you need to love your body. A good way to do this is to have a carefully planned timetable and make sure that you block out times for eating and resting before deciding what else you can fit in.

Some of my other needs (which may be yours too) include:

- fun social interaction
- a safe and warm home environment
- enough money to not be constantly worrying about it

- touch
- anxiety control methods
- a high level of structure: what I do when to be carefully planned out in advance
- acceptance, not judgement
- to work at a pace that is okay for me and to be able to take breaks
- to talk to my safe people when I am upset about something
- not to be keeping any dark secrets to myself.

Dark secrets make me feel ashamed. The feeling of fear of telling someone else is actually not as bad as the feeling of shame – and the feeling of fear is only temporary, before you tell someone, but the feeling of shame is lifelong, if you do not.

Sometimes, what you need is in conflict with another person's needs. For example, my boss needs me to do a lot of typing. But I need to do my typing at a pace that I can cope with and that does not make my stomach hurt. In cases of conflict, it is important to (a) not neglect or fail to notice your need altogether, and (b) to communicate what you need. I am learning that if I communicate my need, I might get it met – at least to some extent. A compromise solution is still better than a completely unmet need. This does not come naturally to me at all, so I need to remember to recognise and communicate my needs.

I am also learning, to my astonishment, that if I communicate my feelings to a safe person, I might actually get my emotional needs met! In the last few weeks, I showed someone that I was feeling sad and I showed someone else that I was feeling traumatised. In both cases, I got a hug, which I did need, without even having to ask! It is, however, also true that communicating feelings to an unsafe person might get you hurt, so I am not advising this one indiscriminately – only with safe people.

3. Give yourself treats

A little child who is always denied what they want is not going to feel loved. Likewise, to feel loved, you can award yourself special treats.

Have a day off. Eat chocolate. Buy some posh food. Spend money on something you really want to do, just for fun.

4. Watch out for 'shoulds' and replace them with kind, forgiving and accepting words

Loving is about accepting and not judging. I have a lot of judgemental, critical thoughts. It can be hard to be aware of these, because many of them are subconscious. But, I can start watching out for the word 'should'. 'Should' is a judgemental, critical word, and it can be replaced by a kinder alternative. For example, 'I am so stupid, I should have remembered to buy the milk,' can be replaced with, 'It's okay, don't worry, I can go back to the shops tomorrow.' There is always a kinder alternative; you just need to work out what it is and then choose it.

5. Talk to yourself in a loving, compassionate way

If you know anyone who talks to you very kindly, gently and non-judgementally, this is what we are trying to copy.

When I say 'talk to yourself', I *do* mean out loud, so this is probably best done in private. Out loud is important. When you talk or write, this comes entirely from your conscious brain: you have decided which words to say and how to say them. When you think, thoughts are swirly – some of them are conscious, but they are mixed with a lot of subconscious thoughts, too. I have been struggling with my thoughts for years. It was a real battle because I was trying my utmost to 'think positive', but I was still feeling very negative. I guess there were a lot of subconscious thoughts sabotaging me. The more that you can keep your words conscious, the more control you have and the more positive they can be. Therefore it is best to talk out loud.

Whatever you decide to say, make it accepting. If you make a mess in the kitchen, say to yourself: 'That is okay, I can clean that up.' When you make mistakes, say that it is okay to make mistakes.

Two of my favourite people call me 'sweetheart' and I really like it. I feel really embarrassed telling you this, but since I am copying how they treat me, I call myself that too. It sounds silly, but it is helping – and I do this in private so no-one hears me!

The tone of your voice is really important. We are going for soft and gentle.

The loudness of your voice is really important. We are going for quiet. Quiet equals nurturing. Loud equals domineering and scary and causes all your defences to fly up. There seems to be an inverse relationship with loudness of voice and loving effectiveness. My heart is most easily reached by the very quietest whisper in my ear.

6. Healing exercise

Lie down on a sofa or somewhere warm and comfortable. I like to lie on my front on my sofa, with a blanket over me and my face pressed a little into the side of the sofa, where the back of it joins the seat. This may sound very weird, but there are reasons. I can wedge my arm into the space between the back of the sofa and the seat, and that creates a nice feeling of deep pressure which I find relaxing. My eyes are closed and the sofa presses gently on my eyelids, so my visual channel is switched off and everything is black and soft. I am about to speak and, in this position, my voice reflects back off the sofa and reaches my ears in a very powerful and direct way. The seat of the sofa exerts a gentle pressure on my windpipe, and I can feel the vibrations of my words inside my body as well as through my ears. I am horizontal so I can relax most of my muscles: I do not need to be holding my shoulders up or back straight, as I would if I were sitting or standing. This makes my breathing easier and more free.

Use a very gentle, soft voice (as described in step 5) and repeat the following out loud: 'I love you. You are safe. I am sorry.'

Also repeat: 'I love you. You are my darling. Everything about you is acceptable.'

Take one breath between each statement. Do this for a few minutes or however long you want to. Do this when you can – ideally every day. You can also say these words to yourself when you are going about your daily life.

Saying these things out loud, and hearing your voice, means that you are both the one doing the loving, and the one receiving the love.

Do not worry if you believe any of these words or not. Eventually, you will probably believe them if you keep going with this. This is not a matter of performing or getting it right. Your only job is to say the words and then see what the result is. In any case, it is a very simple exercise and only takes a few minutes – so it is worth a shot, right?

Do not worry about, or judge, anything that might happen during this exercise. You might experience some emotions. This is okay. It is okay to feel emotions and all emotions are fine.

This was what happened the first time I did this. For the first set of these words, I certainly did not believe that I loved myself, and I hardly ever felt safe. I cried a bit at these statements. 'I am sorry' seemed to trigger something very deep and I cried a lot. I do not know what this was about. Crying is a good sign. Crying is healing. As I did this, lots of tension went away from my back muscles, my ribs got unfrozen (they are usually pretty rigid) and I was able to breathe properly. You do not have to understand what is being healed or what emotions are being let out. I know that when my body relaxes in that way that some inner bit of my heart is being reached.

The second set of words were given to me by my safe person; she said they were from God. When I first heard the 'darling' bit, I cried a lot because my thoughts immediately responded that I was no-one's darling. It was a completely new concept.

However, after some practice at saying these things to myself, I am starting to believe that all these statements are true and I am actually starting to feel that I love myself.

Many people struggle with loving themselves. It is not easy, especially if we have experienced a lot of rejection or abuse in the past, but it is perhaps the best thing we can do for ourselves. You do not have to do it my way – you might already have found your own way. I do not know if it is possible to love yourself without other people loving you first; even if it is, it would certainly be much harder. Therefore, you might want to get the support network stuff sorted out first and to choose trust, honesty and vulnerability with your safe people. It is much easier to love yourself once you already have evidence from outside of yourself that you are lovable.

PART 2

Being Safe with Men
Protecting Yourself, Making Informed Choices and Acting on Your Choices

CHAPTER 4

Understanding the
Female and Male Bodies

Some of the language I am going to use for Part 2 of this book is a wee bit technical, and it includes a number of terms that I did not really know or understand, so before we get into a muddle, here are diagrams of the external male and female sexual body parts:

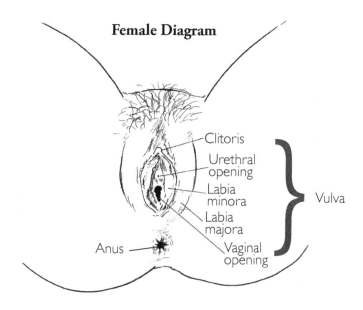

Female Diagram

Clitoris

Urethral
opening

Labia
minora

Labia
majora

Vulva

Anus

Vaginal
opening

Male Diagram

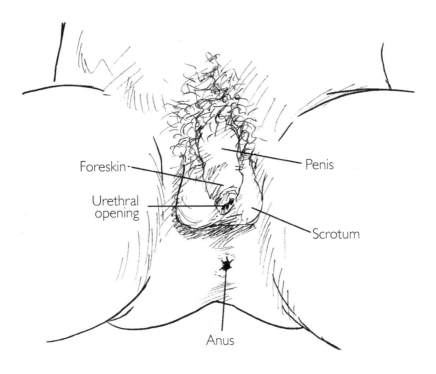

Foreskin
Urethral opening
Penis
Scrotum
Anus

It is sometimes hard to understand how two-dimensional diagrams relate to real life, so I will explain a bit more.

The female body

In the area usually underneath your knickers, there are essentially three openings. Two of these (the vaginal opening and the anus) are larger; the third (the urethral opening) is tiny (see female diagram).

The vaginal opening is found between your legs. If you have ever inserted a tampon, that is the opening that we are talking about. It opens up into the vagina, which is the passageway that leads inside your body to the internal sex organs. The vagina is very stretchy, to allow the passage of a baby during childbirth; it is therefore sometimes referred to as 'the birth canal'. The vaginal opening may not be immediately visible when you look for it, because it is likely to be covered over by the labia majora and the labia minora (see female diagram). 'Labia' is Latin for 'lips'. The labia majora and labia minora generally protect and cover both the vaginal and urethral openings. They can be differently shaped on different people. In the diagram, the person's legs are spread and I reckon the labia minora will have been gently pulled apart to show these two openings (the fingers doing this are not shown), and you will probably need to do that too, to see and access your own vaginal opening.

The urethral opening (the passage from the bladder where your urine comes out) is slightly further towards the front of your body than the vaginal opening, but this is such a small opening that you will not get it confused with the vaginal opening.

The anus (the opening that your faeces come out of) is further towards the back of your body.

So, basically, I consider the vaginal opening to be the big opening between my legs that is covered by the labia, and the anus to be the big opening at the back, and I ignore the urethral opening as too small to notice. If you want, you can find out where these parts are on you by examining your own body. You might find that a mirror helps you to see better.

The clitoris is a small, soft, sensitive bump in front of the vaginal opening, where the labia minora join together. It is about the size and shape of a pea, although the size varies between individual women/ girls. It is, in some ways, the equivalent of a man's penis; when an embryo has only just been formed, you cannot tell at first whether it is a girl or a boy. In the early stages of development, under the influence of hormones, part of the embryo's genitals become a penis, if it is a boy, or a clitoris, if it is a girl.

The clitoris is very sensitive to touch, as it has a lot of nerve endings, and is thought to be the organ most responsible for sexual sensations in women. It can be stimulated (by you or someone else) by touching or stroking it and the area nearby; sexually arousing yourself or someone else by touching the genitals is called masturbation (see Chapter 5). In penis-vaginal sex, the clitoris might become stimulated indirectly because it is very close to the internal vaginal wall. Most women need the clitoris to be stimulated in order to achieve an orgasm during sex or masturbation (see the section at the end of this chapter for a definition of orgasm).

The term 'vulva' means the female's external sex organs, or genitalia, and this includes the vaginal opening, the urethral opening, the labia majora, the labia minora and the clitoris – so, basically, all the externally visible parts that we have discussed here and which are shown in the diagram, except for the anus.

The male body

I will now explain some of the male sexual organs (see male diagram).

The penis is elongate and approximately sausage-shaped. It has a shaft and an enlarged tip. The tip is called the 'glans penis'. The penis can be erect or not erect (flaccid). The penis becomes erect when the man is sexually aroused.

The foreskin is a retractable fold of skin and mucous membrane that covers the glans penis when the penis is flaccid. When the penis is erect, the foreskin retracts to reveal the glans penis. The outside of the foreskin is skin. The inside of the foreskin is a mucous membrane, like the inside of the mouth. This helps the foreskin to move relative to the penis by providing a slightly slippery surface, with less friction than there would otherwise be, skin on skin.

The urethral opening is in the tip of the penis. It carries urine along the urethra from the bladder when the man goes to the toilet. This same passage also carries semen in sexual activity. Semen is a fluid which typically contains sperm cells. One male sperm cell is needed to fertilise a female's egg to make an embryo.

The scrotum is a pouch-like structure that hangs behind the penis. It holds and protects the testes (internal, and therefore not labelled in the diagram). The testes are glands that produce semen, sperm cells and hormones, including testosterone. There is an internal passage (also not shown) which connects the testes to the urethra.

The anus is further towards the back of the body than the penis and the scrotum, and is the passage that faeces come out of.

That is the diagrams explained. Now for a quick definition…

Orgasm

An orgasm is a powerful feeling of pleasure which can happen during sexual activity (see NHS Choices 2010a). During an orgasm, the heart beats faster and the breathing gets quicker. Both men and women can have orgasms. Sex and orgasms are good things in loving, committed, adult relationships. Not everyone experiences orgasms, and that's okay; but if this is a problem, a doctor might be able to suggest a solution.

When a woman has an orgasm, her genital muscles contract and her hips may jerk. A woman can experience an orgasm if her clitoris is repeatedly touched/massaged – either by herself or someone else – or through other types of sexual activity.

When the man has an orgasm, he ejaculates semen from his penis. A man can experience an orgasm when his penis is repeatedly touched/stroked – either by himself or someone else – or through other types of sexual activity.

Okay, that is the technical bit out of the way, so let us now get on to the topic of boyfriends.

CHAPTER 5

Boyfriends

What is a boyfriend?

I always thought a boyfriend was someone who you went on dates with. I guess this is partly true. But you can date someone many times and still not feel emotionally close to them. This was certainly my experience. I knew that I was hiding something from my ex-boyfriend and that I was pretending, but at the time, I did not know that I was an Aspie and I had no clue about what I could be hiding or why. I definitely felt like I was playing some sort of role that I was not too keen on playing. We did a lot of French kissing. I did not like it very much, but I thought that was what you were supposed to do, so I did it. I thought that with time and effort, we would grow closer, but we did not. It did not occur to me that I was simply with the wrong person.

One of the things that I was, in fact, hiding was the fact that I was rather bored with all the kissing and I also do not really like the feeling of having someone's tongue inside my mouth. I did not really want to do it, but I was unable to tell him that due to my lack of boundaries and difficulty with saying 'no'. I was also particularly afraid that I was clearly very weird indeed for not enjoying it and I thought (wrongly) that I did not have any right to say 'no', because I thought that kissing is in the 'job description' of girlfriend. Everyone else seemed to be doing it. I was also acting in a way that did not match my feelings (French kissing implies an intimacy that I did not feel at all), which also seemed to me like a lie, and that was bothering me a lot.

I now realise that what a boyfriend is would be better defined in terms of emotional closeness. A boyfriend is someone who you are having an intimate one-on-one relationship with, who knows and likes the real you. I guess the poor chap I was with did not have much of a chance, because I never showed him the real me. A boyfriend is someone you feel comfortable enough with to show them the real you. And that has a lot to do with genuinely loving yourself first.

Who is not a boyfriend?

A person is *not* a boyfriend if he is:

- a man who is much older than you (generally speaking, although some women do choose much older men). If you are 16, for example, a 40-year-old is probably not a good choice for a boyfriend, and I would be highly suspicious of his motives

- a man with a specific role in your life, such as your teacher, lecturer, tutor, support worker, social worker, policeman, priest, mentor, sports coach, etc.

- a member of your family – for example, your father, step-father, uncle, grandfather or brother

- a man who is married to someone else or who is someone else's boyfriend.

This list is not exhaustive, but it has the main types that I can think of. It is really important to remember this list, because bad people might lie to you. If any of these types of men tell you that they are your boyfriend (or ask to be your boyfriend), tell you that you want to be their girlfriend or that you want to have sex with them, then they are lying and you need to not believe them. You need to tell someone in your support network what they have said so that they can help you.

If any of these types of men touch your breasts, inner thighs, your bottom or any of the area usually covered by your knickers, or if any of these types of men have sex with you (I will explain the full definition of what this means later on), then this is wrong of them and you need to get help, fast. By 'touch' here, I do not mean an accidental touch – for example, if someone brushes past you. I mean a stroking or another sort of deliberate touch. This is an extremely bad situation and some of these examples are sexual abuse. It is absolutely *not* okay to be happening, under any circumstances. If this is currently happening to you, or has happened in the past, I am really sorry. You need to find someone in your support network to talk to about this. If a member of your family is doing any of these things to you, then you should tell someone in your support network who is not in your family. It is extremely important to remember you *must* communicate about this. If you have promised to keep what is happening a secret, then the rule is you *must* break this promise. It is okay to break a promise when it is a bad promise and this is a very bad promise. It is almost certain that you were forced or coerced into making it.

Sometimes, girls/women do not want to communicate that any of these things are happening to them because they feel afraid, embarrassed, ashamed, guilty and/or stupid. Whilst these are very understandable feelings, which many people have in these circumstances, these feelings are very bad reasons not to communicate. If anything like this is happening to you, it is *not* your fault, you did not cause it to happen and you are not going to be told off or blamed. It is crucial that you communicate about this, so that you can stop it happening. Do not give in to your embarrassment. If you do not communicate, it will go on happening and you will get hurt, possibly emotionally and physically. If you do not communicate, you are protecting the man who is abusing you and you are putting yourself in danger of further harm. If you do not communicate, other people will also be in danger from this man.

What is a bad boyfriend?

A bad boyfriend is one who acts in one or more of the following ways:

- He lies to you. You might find this out if he is telling you different stories at different times, these stories contradicting each other. If you challenge him about this and he cannot give you an explanation, or if you end up just feeling very confused by him, his behaviour and his stories, I would take this as an indication he is probably lying. If you want a second opinion about this, tell someone you trust about your situation and see what they think. A lot of non-spectrum people are good at detecting liars and manipulators and could be really helpful here.

- He steals from you, or is using you to get money.

- He is only interested in having sex with you or doing other physical stuff but is not interested in your personality or the real you.

- He treats you nicely and horribly in different situations, or treats you nicely at first but then treats you badly later on.

- He is physically violent to you or threatens you with violence. This means someone who, on purpose, ever hits you, punches you, slaps you, kicks you, pinches you, bites you, burns you, bruises you, gives you Chinese burns, strangles you, hits you with a stick or other object, or anything similar to any of these. These things are never okay. If anyone does anything like this to you, the rule is you need to get help fast and you need to get out of the relationship. It does not matter if you like him or not. It does not matter if you love him. Anyone who is being violent to you is abusing you, and you need to make this stop. This kind of behaviour is often called 'domestic abuse'. One reason that you have to get help and to get out of the relationship is that if you do nothing, the physical abuse is likely to continue and to get worse and your life may be in danger. It is extremely important to get far away from anyone in your life who is being violent to you and for you to get help. This is not negotiable. In order to get help, you will probably need to tell someone. You could start off by telling someone in your support network, and they could help you decide if you need to go to the police. There are women's shelters where you can go to get out of an unsafe environment. It might seem that you have no options, but you always have a choice. Use that choice to escape, no matter what.

- He forces you to have sex or do any sexual activity with him if you do not want to. Again, use your choice to escape, no matter what.

- He causes you to feel bad about yourself. I do not mean someone who says a comment that you take the wrong way by accident – because that is going to happen with everyone. I mean someone who makes fun of you in a nasty way; or someone who tells you that you are fat or ugly or unlovable or any other insulting thing. It is sometimes hard to know when people are joking. So if this just happens once, it might be a misinterpretation. But if this man repeatedly says derogatory things to you, then he is a bad boyfriend. There could be a few reasons for his nasty behaviour. It might be about him trying to gain power over you. It might be because he feels insecure about himself and he is trying to make himself feel better by putting you down. He might be trying to gain popularity by making other people laugh at you. But whatever the reason, this behaviour is not okay as it is damaging to your self-esteem. Just because someone says something does not mean that it is true. If someone does say something like this to you, it is very important not to believe it. We always have a choice about other people's statements. We can accept them as true or we can reject them as false.

- He has another girlfriend, fiancé or wife as well as you. This is unfair behaviour towards everyone involved. Boyfriend/girlfriend relationships are supposed to be one-on-one.

If you are going out with someone like this, I would advise you to get out of the relationship and have nothing more to do with him. You are far better off being alone than being with anyone who would do any of these things to you. You are precious and you are worth so much more than that.

It can be really hard to tell who is a good person and who is trustable from who is not. I like to think that I am a good judge of character, but if you are an Aspie like me, this is actually a really hard thing to be. I am discovering that I am not nearly as good at this as I have previously believed. Also, boyfriends who initially seem nice can turn nasty later on, because niceness can easily be faked by lying and pretending. It is a good plan to ask your friends or your support network what they think of the person you are dating. They might be able to judge character well and to keep you from making a terrible mistake. Of course, not everyone is horrible, and I have known many more nice people than horrible ones, but the people who are horrible are very good at spotting people who are vulnerable, like us Aspies.

What are people who are not your boyfriend *not* allowed to do?

A man who is not your boyfriend is not allowed to:

- kiss you by putting his tongue in your mouth (French kissing)
- expose the area usually underneath his underwear so that you can see it (i.e. 'flashing')
- touch your breasts, either through your clothes or underneath your clothes
- touch your thighs, especially not the inside part of your thighs
- touch any part of your body with his crotch area, clothed or otherwise
- put his hands between your body and your knickers or to remove your knickers.
- touch your vulva or anus or anywhere around these areas, either through your clothes or underneath your clothes, with his mouth, tongue, fingers, penis or any other part of his body or with any other object
- touch the inside of your vagina or anus with his finger, tongue or penis or with any other object
- have sex with you.

All of the above are sexual acts, which is why men who are not your boyfriend are not allowed to do them. You need to learn this list of rules. Even if you are with someone you really trust who is not your boyfriend, he is still not allowed to do any of these things. This can be confusing if you are just not expecting it, as people who are not boyfriends can seem really 'safe' – you are not even thinking about sex around them and so you are not on your guard. You might assume that they would not do anything wrong. But, unfortunately, this is not always the case. It can be very confusing if the wrong word is used to describe what is happening. For example, it is very easy for something described as a 'massage', in which it is normal for someone to be touching your body, to stray over into areas where touch is not allowed. This can also happen when you are dancing with someone or hugging. If you misclassify what is going on as something that is not sexual, for example labelling it as 'massage', 'dancing' or 'hugging' then you might not even think about the boundary stuff that you probably would realise was relevant and would consider if you were thinking in terms of boyfriends. Try to think concretely about what is actually happening. Also, it can just be a question of a few centimetres between touch that is safe and okay and touch that is not, and some stuff is borderline.

Where I usually go wrong is that I think first about the context – who I am with, in what context I know them, and what the activity is called, and then assume what is happening cannot be sexual, and I have made quite a few mistakes in that way. However, the right way to do it is to think first about the area of your body being touched and if it is your breasts, your inner thighs or the area usually covered by your knickers, then this is probably sexual, no matter who is doing it – male or female, child, teenager or adult. An exception is that babies naturally root towards anyone's breasts when they are trying to feed and this is not sexual.

Another exception to this is that doctors and some other health professionals are allowed to touch you in some of these ways, if it is to do with examining you or treating you for a health problem that you have presented with. For example, if you tell your doctor about a pain in your breast, they will probably need to see your breast without any clothes on and touch your breast. But there should always be a good reason for this. If you tell your doctor about a pain in your finger, they are then not allowed to look at or touch your breasts. It is exceedingly rare that any doctor would abuse your trust, so it is okay to trust doctors. What a doctor might do is to have someone else in the room with them (for example, behind a screen) to ensure that everything is done properly. If your doctor is proposing to do any of these things, just make sure you understand the reason and that it makes logical sense. If you are not sure, say 'no' for now and that you want to think about it and decide later. Leave the appointment and check out their proposal with someone in your support network or by doing your own research. You can always go back to the doctor later if you decide that it is okay. You can always ask to see a female doctor if you feel safer and more able to trust them.

What acts are not allowed for anyone to do?

Here are some more rules which apply to everyone, whether or not they are your boyfriend, your friend or a member of your family.

It is not allowed for anyone to:

- lock you in a cupboard with them

- lock you in a room with them against your will (apart from acts of safety and/or discipline by genuinely loving people, such as sharing a hotel room with a safe person and locking the room to prevent intruders, or a parent giving you time to calm down as a reasonable consequence for some behaviour in order to protect and help you and/or others)
- be violent towards you, or to hurt you on purpose on any part of your body
- force you to undress in front of them
- see you without any clothes on (or with some clothes on but your breasts, vulva and/or bottom area exposed) if you do not want them to. This is not allowed whether they do this secretly or openly
- touch your breasts, vulva and/or bottom if you do not want them to, either through your clothes, underneath your clothes or without your clothes on
- take photographs of your breasts, vulva or bottom without any clothes on, or whilst you are in your underwear, without your consent
- force you to watch pornography (for example, a DVD of people having sex)
- force you to take part in the making of pornography (for example, by videoing you without clothes on or whilst performing any sexual act)
- force you to touch the sexual areas of their body with any part of your body
- force you to touch the sexual areas of someone else's body, with any part of your body
- force you to take a shower or a bath with them
- force their way into a bathroom with you or to watch you in the bathroom
- put their finger, tongue, penis, or any other body part or object into your vagina or anus if you do not agree to this
- have sex with you if you do not agree to this.

Equally, it is not allowed for you to do any of these things to anyone else.

Any agreement that you do give must be because you genuinely want to and not because you are being forced, coerced or manipulated into agreeing. It is not allowed for anyone to threaten you or blackmail you in order to obtain your agreement. For example, it is not allowed for someone to say: 'If you do not allow me to do such-and-such to you, I will go and do it to someone else instead'; and it is not allowed for anyone to threaten to hurt you or anyone you love if you do not comply.

Some of these things are also not allowed if you are younger than the 'age of consent' in your country, even if you do agree. There is more information about the age of consent in Chapter 10.

When I say 'not allowed' here, I mean that these things should never happen and are wrong. However, just because something is not allowed, does not mean that it will not happen. I am telling you so that you will know that these things are wrong. I am not telling you this in order to try to make you feel guilty if any of these things have happened to you. For example, if someone forces you to have sex with them, or if someone forces you to abuse someone else, these things are not allowed but they are not your fault and you do not have to feel guilty about them. The person who is wrong is the one who made you do them, not you.

You need to remember these rules very hard, even if someone is telling you other rules. It is difficult to not believe what we are being told. Often, it seems like other people are a lot more right than us, and we should be 'good girls' who do what we are told. It can often be fine to trust other people's judgement. But some people are bad and will lie to you in order to get something that they want from you – for example, your compliance for their sexual gratification. You need to be very sure that *you* know these rules, so that you do not get convinced by someone else lying and telling you other rules.

One thing I find difficult is that someone might not tell you what they are going to do, ask your permission, or warn you, before they are already doing it. I might be able to give a very clear answer if someone actually asked me first, whether I wanted them to touch me in a certain way or not. But, if the person does not ask and then they just do it anyway, because of my surprise, confusion, embarrassment and being in the middle of an awkward situation, I find it much harder to work out if I am okay with it or not, to work out what to do to stop it and to be brave enough to stop it. This is why this needs some good, clear thought beforehand. The more you think out beforehand, the less you will have to work out in a stressful situation.

Why these things are not allowed

Warning: you may find some of this next section to be shocking.
I have not always understood why some of these things are wrong. My definition of things that are wrong is usually measured by whether I am hurting anyone else or being hurt, but someone touching certain parts of my body feels nice and it does not feel like I am being hurt – nor does it feel like I am hurting anyone else by permitting it. So, I am just left with a vague feeling that society thinks some of these things are wrong, but I do not tend to do or not do things just because society says so. I need a better explanation. So, I have found this very confusing. I think I have now worked out why these things are wrong, and here is my best explanation.

Sexual pleasure

Your breasts and the area usually under your knickers have a lot of nerve endings and are very sensitive to touch. These are deeply intimate and deeply private parts of your body. Being touched in these places feels pleasurable to most women and this pleasure is a sexual pleasure. I have not always recognised this as sexual pleasure in the past. Being touched in general feels very nice for me and there is no big flashing sign that comes up saying: 'Warning – this is sexual pleasure' when touch strays over into these areas.

I gave a definition of an orgasm in Chapter 4. It is one type of sexual pleasure and is a very powerful feeling. It is also quite addictive. Our brains are geared up to seek pleasure and to avoid pain, and an orgasm is intensely pleasurable – to some people, the most pleasurable body sensation that there is.

Sexual pleasure is a good thing in general and it is natural to seek it out, just like everyone does with other pleasurable experiences.

Sexual pleasure is a wonderful thing in the right situation – for example, when it is experienced in the context of an adult, stable, loving relationship with someone who loves and cherishes you, and who you love in return. It can help couples to feel more in love and connected with each other, and is a giving of the self on a very deep level. Sexual pleasure is an incentive for people to have sex and therefore to produce children – so the human race can continue.

It is also important to understand that both children and adults can experience sexual pleasure outside the context of the sort of relationship described above, whether or not they are in a relationship. Children and adults may touch their own genitals and experience very pleasant sensations. Touching or rubbing the genital area so that it feels good is called masturbation. Masturbation is an okay and a healthy thing to do in general, as long as you are not doing it compulsively or addictively. Some children do it because it feels good to them, because they are curious or to provide comfort when they are upset, tired or bored, and I think adults who masturbate probably have very similar reasons, as well as finding it generally enjoyable and relaxing. However, there is a very important social rule (for children and adults) that masturbation is only ever done in a private place. A suitable private place is in your bedroom, with the door closed.

Another crucial social rule is that you do not discuss masturbation with most people. It might possibly be okay to discuss it with a parent, someone who is like a parent to you or with an extremely close friend (but even then it is a bit risky because most people would not talk about this, so you have to really trust them and use your own judgement about whether this is safe), but it is not okay to discuss it with work colleagues, most of your friends or most people that you know. Also, even if you are with someone that you are very close to and you trust very much, you need to wait until you are alone with them and cannot be overheard; do not talk about it in a public place where someone else could hear you. Sometimes I choose not to follow some social rules, but *not* in this case. These rules are non-optional and life could get unpleasant and embarrassing for you if you break them.

If you choose to masturbate in private that is perfectly fine; it is not wrong and there is nothing to feel guilty or ashamed about. This is really important to know because, often, other things that are kept secret do seem to be shameful, but this is absolutely not the case here. People sometimes pick up feelings of shame about masturbation from society in general or from their upbringing (for example, if a parent sees their young child touching their genitals out of curiosity and reacts in a harsh way to it, that can teach the child that masturbation is something to be ashamed of), but this is one of these cases where society and other people are not right. Some people choose not to masturbate and that is equally okay. This is a matter of personal choice.

Sometimes young children explore each other's bodies, and may experience pleasurable feelings through these games. This is often just a normal stage of development, and is harmless as long as the children are similar in age and development, and are not being threatened or coerced by each other.

When sexual pleasure is confusing

Sexual pleasure is not a good thing in every situation, even though it might feel very nice indeed and even if you are not physically hurting anyone or being hurt. A problem can come if you experience sexual pleasure with someone else who is inappropriate or even bad. Sexual pleasure affects your brain and your emotions. It is deeply intimate and personal, and you do not want to give your deep self to just anyone.

Examples of bad situations include a 13-year-old boy touching a seven-year-old girl's vagina; a 40-year-old man touching a teenager's breasts or having sex with her; any adult performing any type of sexual act on a child; and anyone having sex with any other person against their will. The first three situations are wrong because they are with dissimilar ages and developments; there is an imbalance of power and they are therefore unsafe. These bad situations are, or are very likely to be, sexual abuse. Another bad situation is if you are feeling confused, scared, threatened or coerced by the other person in any way. It is not always easy to know how you are feeling. If you are having trouble identifying your feelings, you can get clues from your body. Clues that you are feeling confused, scared or sad include your heart beating faster, or if you are sweating, crying or shaking.

Sexual pleasure may still feel (at least partly) very nice, even if you experience it with a bad person. It is very confusing to associate very strong feelings of sexual pleasure with a situation in which you are not a willing participant, with someone you do not really like or love, trust or even know very well, or someone who may be hurting you as well as giving you this sexual pleasure. This can make you very vulnerable, not just emotionally, but also physically, including putting you at risk of sexually transmitted infections and pregnancy if you fail to take precautions.

What you feel and think makes connections in your brain. There is a risk that you may begin to make unhelpful and destructive connections between feelings that are pleasurable and acts or situations that are bad for you or for someone else. You do not want to associate the lovely things that sex can be in an adult, loving, committed relationship and the feelings of sexual pleasure (which are good and right in this context) with any bad sexual experiences which were against your will, when you were too young, or which happened in a context in which you were not loved, cherished and safe. You do not want sex in a stable and loving relationship to remind you of bad experiences and trigger some bad memories.

Sexual acts make you very vulnerable to being hurt because the most vulnerable and sensitive parts of your body are being exposed to someone else. If someone else is touching these vulnerable parts of you, they have some control over your body and your mind. This can feel very scary if you are not with someone who loves you, or if you are not ready for it.

Just be aware, though, that experiencing sexual pleasure with someone who is not your boyfriend/husband is not always an abusive situation. In my case, some of these times were not very wise, in retrospect, but I did consent, and they were fairly innocent and definitely non-abusive.

Sexual abuse

The dark side of orgasms and other forms of sexual pleasure, however, is that these can be misused as part of sexual abuse. This part is very difficult for me to write, but Aspies need the truth, so here goes…

Sexual acts can awaken your sexuality in an adult way before you are ready for this. Young children are definitely not ready for sexual acts. It is always wrong for an adult to do a sexual act with a child. Some Aspie women may not be ready for such sexual encounters, either, if they are still emotionally very young. I think that chronological age is not the best measure of actual age when it comes to Aspies, because I believe we develop on a different timescale to others.

People who sexually abuse others can use sexual pleasure as a way of manipulating others. This is pure evil.

Your body responds to certain types of touch automatically, like turning on a switch, even if your mind hates what is happening. If a particular action happens to your body, your body provides a particular response. If your knee is hit a certain way, your leg does a jumping reflex. If a light shines in your eyes, your pupils get smaller. If you hear a loud noise, your muscles tense.

Likewise, your body responds to sexual touch in ways that you cannot control. People getting sexually abused, even in an aggressive, violent way, can experience orgasms and other sexual pleasure because this is an automatic, touch-triggered response. You can be forced to have an orgasm by someone else, even if you do not want them to do this, even if you hate them and even if they are forcing their touch on you and you cannot get away. Not only women, but girls, young girls and even toddlers can be forced to have orgasms, which is so horrifying that I am struggling to type this.

If you are sexually abused by someone touching your breasts or the area usually underneath your knickers, you may find it at least partly enjoyable, because being gently touched in these areas does feel very nice for most girls/women. If your clitoris is stroked or massaged repeatedly, you will probably be forced to orgasm sooner or later. If you experience any pleasure by this touch, or if you are forced to orgasm, *you are being manipulated into thinking that you enjoy it*. Your abuser might directly lie to you that you wanted the sexual abuse to happen, and argue that your pleasure or the fact that they made you orgasm is evidence. But even if they do not say it, you may be very confused about your feelings of pleasure and think this anyway – it is a very natural conclusion. Since brains are programmed to seek pleasure, some people may unwittingly ask for a sensory experience to be repeated, perhaps without recognising it as being sexual. If you have been abused and found any level of pleasure in it, or if you afterwards asked for this again, do not worry, this was the effect of the manipulation and was not your fault. You are not guilty. *Not guilty.*

Conflicting feelings

Sexual abuse typically causes the person being abused to have conflicting feelings, which may include pleasure, wanting it, not wanting it, fear, pain, hate, self-hate, guilt, shame, and, of course, confusion due to having all these mixed up and contradictory feelings; I will explain more about this in Chapter 13. The fact that someone who sexually abuses others knows this and intentionally wants to cause this is something so evil that I could have never imagined it.

A person sexually abusing you might want to make you experience an orgasm or other sexual pleasure to awaken your sexuality before you are ready for it; to make you feel guilty, ashamed and responsible for the abuse so that you will not tell anyone what they did; to gain your compliance and to control you, so you are more likely to do what they want; to be cruel; to set up a conflict and confusion in your mind as to whether you wanted them to abuse you or not; and/ or to get you addicted to orgasms. It is even more damaging when this is done to a child, because their brain is still young and forming and this can make the addiction issue worse. All of this is pure evil on the abuser's part.

If you are hit by someone (physical abuse), this is awful but at least there is no way that you could think that you enjoyed being hit and there is no way that anyone else could convince you that you enjoyed it or wanted it.

But in contrast, if you are sexually abused, any pleasure that you are forced to experience can make you think that you enjoyed it and can make you want it to happen again; you are manipulated into thinking you enjoyed or wanted the abuse. Anyone sexually abusing you is committing an enormous act of violation of your body and this act is also an enormous lie which gets directly into your mind.

Therefore, there are some situations where your body can feel very nice, but which are still wrong. Remembering some of these rules should help. Basically, you need to decide things with your brain and not your body. Just because something feels nice does not always mean that it is okay to be doing it. This particularly applies to any kind of sexual touching happening with anyone who is not your boyfriend. If any of these things happen to you, try to get the person to stop by saying 'No' in a loud voice and by pushing them away. Get away as soon as you can. Tell someone you trust and get safe. If the first person you tell does not help, keep telling other people you trust until you are safe. Never, ever go back to the person who did this to you. To remember what to do, think: 'No. Go. Tell.' Repeat this to yourself so that you memorise it. Do not worry if you make any mistakes – it is okay to make mistakes and this stuff is hard for anyone, let alone Aspies. You are not guilty, the situation is not your fault and you have nothing to be ashamed about.

I am really sorry that I had to include this bit and I hope you are feeling okay after having read it. I felt traumatised after researching some of this. I had no idea that such evil and manipulation existed. This might be a good time to take a break. You could eat some chocolate and perhaps get a hug.

Protecting yourself

The good news is there are practical things you can do for yourself right now which will decrease your likelihood of getting into abusive situations. Sexual abusers are looking for girls and women who are ill-informed, isolated and lonely; in other words, people they can 'groom' by befriending them and making them feel special. This was a very good description of me as a teenager, and in fact I think this 'grooming' process was exactly what happened to me, although I am only just understanding this now. You can help protect yourself by not being like I was. You can be well informed – you have already made a very good start on that by reading this book. This is really important, because the first obstacle is knowing right from wrong. You can be connected and not isolated by making and developing your own support network. You can find nice people who genuinely love you and who will tell you that you are special and precious, so you will not be susceptible to false flattery by a bad person. You can practise communicating about sexuality, boyfriends and this whole potentially embarrassing subject area with the safest people in your life. This is difficult, but it builds character and courage and the rewards are intimacy, knowledge and confidence. This will get you even better informed and, if you are already used to talking about sex as a normal topic and not avoiding it as a taboo area, then if, later on, you do have a bad, abusive experience, when you come to tell your safest person, although this will still be difficult, at least broaching the entire topic will not be entirely new to you; you will have a vocabulary to do it with and the necessary level of trust and security in your relationship with your safe person.

Therefore, there are lots of things that you can do to make yourself safer than I ever was, and become a more confident, secure and happy person in the process.

Some quick, standard responses

If a man who is not your boyfriend:

- asks if you want a massage, the answer is 'no'

- asks if he can touch your leg, breasts, chest, vulva or bottom, the answer is 'no'

- wants to sleep in the same double bed as you, the answer is 'no'. This is because you are too vulnerable to him, should he turn out to be untrustworthy and abusive. You do not want him to touch you or have sex with you whilst you are asleep

- does any of these things without asking, your response is to get away from him as quickly as you can if it is safe to do so.

If you are with your boyfriend and:

- you are kissing and he asks if you want to go somewhere more comfortable, he is not really thinking about your comfort but he is using an indirect code which means going into a bedroom and having sex. So, if you do not want to do this, then the answer is 'no'

- he suggests going back to your place or his for coffee, he does not really mean to drink coffee, but he means kissing/touching or sex. So, if you do not want to do this, the answer is 'no'. You need to be very sure that you can trust a man completely before you are alone with him.

What *are* boyfriends allowed to do?

Boyfriends are only allowed to do what you are comfortable with, because your skin and your body belong to you and are within your boundaries. Therefore, allowing a boyfriend to touch your body is within your control and responsibility and any permission you do allow is a gift to be freely given if you wish, or not given, if you do not wish. You should not give such a gift because of fear – for example, that he will leave you if you do not give it.

Boyfriends are not allowed to have sex with you if one or both of you are under the 'age of consent'. The 'age of consent' means the age at which someone can legally consent to sexual activity, and is different in different countries. I will explain the age of consent in more detail in Chapter 10. The rest of this section assumes that you and your boyfriend are both over the age of consent.

To what extent you allow someone else access to your body is a matter of how much you are willing to give. This is a very personal decision and lots of people have different ideas. I have always thought that if you do not love someone, you should not have sex with them. For some people, they would not want to have sex with anyone before being married to them. But within this category of people, there is a range of how much sexual touch they will allow from a boyfriend, from no sexual touch at all until marriage, to everything but penis-vaginal or anal sex. Then there are other people entirely who have sex with people they have only just met. Some people have sex with their friends, with no long-term commitment. Some people have several sexual partners at any one time. You will need to think about and decide upon what is okay with you or not. Sex is not risk-free (I will explain this in more detail in Chapter 8). If you are not sure, it is probably best to err on the side of caution and do less rather than more.

While this is a bit of a generalisation, it would be fair to say that quite often men want sex more than girls/women do. If you are dating a man, he might want to have sex with you before you feel ready for this, or do some sexual activities that you do not want to do. This is something you could both discuss. Words are important here. A man is unlikely to guess that you might find it difficult to say 'no' to him, and it is impossible for him to read your mind and realise that you do not want to do something if you do not communicate 'no' in some way to him. If a man does (or starts to do) something that you are not comfortable with, you have a choice to ask him to stop.

So, it is your job to work out what you want to do, and what you do not want to do, and then communicate this to the man. If you are with a good man, he will respect your wishes here. You could say 'no' with words, or by physically moving his hand or other body part away. If you do not do either of these things, the man is going to think that you are okay with what he is doing and that you are communicating that it is fine for him to carry on.

What you do, and do not, want to do with a man is something you might want to discuss with a woman in your support network. It is a good idea to think this out beforehand. When you are already in a tricky situation, it is really hard to make the right decision, because you do not have a long time with no distractions to think about what to do. Also, be sure you know what to do to enforce your boundaries by saying 'no' – because if you do not, you might end up doing stuff that you do not want to do, which might freak you out.

CHAPTER 6

Kissing

There are two main types of kissing; you can do it with a closed mouth (on someone's cheek or mouth) or an open mouth, where each person has their tongue inside the other person's mouth. I will call the closed mouth version 'friendly kissing' because that seems to me a good description, and the open mouth version 'French kissing', because this is what it is usually called. To start with, the first point of potential confusion is that French kissing is not only done by French people, and neither is it the only way that French people kiss! So, 'French kissing' is just a name and basically you should ignore the literal interpretation here.

Friendly kissing (the closed mouth kind)

Friendly kissing varies a lot between cultures and within cultures. Some families friendly kiss each other, for example, on the cheek, and some families never kiss. For example, your mum might kiss you on the cheek if she is that kind of mum. To my horror, I found that in Scotland, after New Year, coming into work, all my colleagues were friendly kissing each other on the cheek in greeting; I was not used to kissing at all, and it was my first day in this workplace. I shrank back against the wall in horror and luckily no-one kissed me!

Britain tends to be a stiff-upper-lip, 'let-us-shake-hands-and-be-quite-stand-offish' culture, compared to a lot of other cultures. For example, French people do friendly kissing on the cheek as a greeting every time they meet their family and friends, just as a way of saying 'hello'. In some parts of France, it is one kiss on each cheek, and other parts of France it is three or four kisses, always alternating cheeks. I went on a French exchange with my school for two weeks when I was 13 and I found all the kissing incredibly embarrassing and awkward at first, but towards the end I got to quite like it. Now, I think the French have definitely got the right idea, because I enjoy physical contact with people and because kissing makes you feel loved – not necessarily in the romantic sense, but in the kind of love that we all need to thrive.

Hugging and friendly kissing can be a bit nerve-wracking, mostly because you have to get intimately close to someone to do these things and it can be a bit hard if, like me, you are a bit dyspraxic and clumsy and struggle to be co-ordinated and to know where all your body parts are. You are close to them, they are close to you, you are moving, they are moving, you are struggling to process the movements of all their body parts and your body parts quickly enough, whilst also trying not to head-butt them, spit on them, hit them on the chin with your shoulder when you cannot see where your shoulder is or where their chin is, hit them or anyone else nearby with your hands or arms, or touch them anywhere inappropriate. I have got all these things wrong at times, but luckily not all at the same time! You also have to judge whether a hug or a kiss is an okay thing to do with any particular person in any particular social situation. Taking the initiative to friendly kiss or hug anyone also goes against all my instincts to be passive, scared and to avoid initiating anything with anyone. However, you do get a bit better with practice (although my dyspraxia is always going to be there), and real friends do not mind if you get things a bit wrong accidentally. It also becomes much easier to do and less scary with practice. I think that friendly kissing and hugging are both very nice and so it is worth being a bit brave, trying it out and practising. Do not worry if you get it a bit wrong. You are not going to seriously injure anyone.

French kissing (the open mouth kind with each person's tongue in the other's mouth)

French kissing is a more sexual kind of kiss and is not allowed between friends or family members, but only with boyfriends/husbands. I was very afraid before I tried it that I would not know how to do it, but it is actually pretty easy, so you do not need to worry about that. They open their mouth, you open your mouth, they put their tongue into your mouth and move it around your tongue and your teeth and you do the same back to them. Apparently, some people find this exquisitely pleasurable, although I do not, and I do not really get what other people see in it. Your partner might be just holding you whilst this is going on, or he might be moving his hands around your body, for example, on your breasts, hips, back and bottom, if you let him. French kissing can be done whilst standing, sitting or lying down. Also, some people have very bad smelling breath, and you might find this really off-putting. When I first met my ex-boyfriend, he was always chewing gum and I thought that was quite a strange thing to do (since I never chew gum), but eventually I realised he was trying to make his breath smell nicer. When he was not chewing gum, he had terribly bad smelling breath. I could not tell him about it (I was too shy), but it was very hard to kiss him when the smell made me feel a bit ill.

If someone's face is looming up at you with their mouth slightly open, they might be going to French kiss you. In my experience, this often happens at the end of a date. If you have decided beforehand that you want to do this, then go right ahead and let them. If you do not want to kiss them in this way, what you can do instead is turn your head so that their mouth will meet your cheek and not your mouth – so you ensure that the kiss is a 'friendly' type, not a 'French' type. I think this is a good way, because it is not a complete rejection of them, and it will probably save them some embarrassment. If the man is a nice person and is not attacking you, turning your cheek towards their kiss sounds like a better plan and a much more proportionate response than punching them, or screaming and running away! However, if they are attacking you, you are allowed to scream, punch, bite, kick and do whatever you can to make sure that you get away.

It was a big surprise to me to learn that you do not have to let someone French kiss you after a date. This was so 'normal' for me (it seemed to be expected every time, with whoever it was), that I had taken it to be a part of what going on the date was, even if it was a first date or a blind date. As usual, I found myself just meeting what I believed was the social expectation, because I thought I had to. However, it is, on the contrary, always okay to say 'no' to this, or any other sexual act that you do not want to do. It is again that issue of boundaries. One of your boundaries is your skin, which defines your body. Anyone French kissing you has their tongue within your body and therefore, very literally and physically, within your boundaries. You are in charge of what is allowed to happen within your boundaries. If you refuse to let someone French kiss you, anyone who does not respect your 'no' here is not a good person. Anyone who does not want to date you again because of this is not the right person for you, so good riddance to them.

My analysis of: 'I went on X number of dates with men, they all stuck their tongue in my mouth at the end of the date, therefore this must be normal and it certainly happens a lot on TV doesn't it?' was wrong because all the data points were taken with men. I have no experiential data on what other girls do in similar circumstances, unless I go around and ask them (which it normally would not occur to me to do). Aspies try very hard to meet other people's social expectations, and usually this is a good thing. But here is one area where you actually need to do the opposite and *not* meet the social expectation if you are not comfortable with anything such as French kissing or touching.

Always remember that French kissing is not allowed between friends or family members, but only with boyfriends/husbands. So, if anyone who is not your boyfriend or husband tries to French kiss you, this is not allowed and is not okay (if they tell you otherwise, they are lying) and you should do anything you can to avoid this and to escape from the situation, unless your life would be in danger by trying to escape.

On the other hand, French kissing is a generally okay thing to do with boyfriends if you definitely want to do it. The first time I kissed a boy in this way, I had a major stress afterwards because I had kissed someone who I did not love. I thought I was the world's biggest slut. My friends laughed like crazy when I told them what I was worrying about. I learned from this that kissing is an okay thing to do and it is all about experimenting and learning. You are not a slut just because you have kissed a boy. It can be part of the 'getting to know each other' process. It is also fine and normal to kiss someone and then wish you had not done so afterwards. Everyone (Aspie or otherwise) makes mistakes in this area. It is okay to make mistakes. Mistakes are valuable learning experiences.

Okay, so that is kissing. But if you are with a boyfriend, he will probably want to have sex with you sooner or later. So, the first question is, what could this mean…?

CHAPTER 7

What is Sex?

It might seem a bit daft that I am including this section, but to my surprise, I really did not know the full definition. I thought that sex had to involve a penis and being completely naked, and my main understanding of it was the penis-vaginal kind that they teach you about in school and that you read about in *The Body Book* or some such children's title that someone gives you when you are around 11, thinking that they have done their duty and that you have now received 'sex education'. But no, there are all sorts, including:

- penis-vaginal sexual intercourse
- fingering (touching inside or around the outside of the vagina or anus)
- oral sex (one person's mouth/tongue stimulating the other person's genitals)
- anal sex (penetration of the anus by a penis or an object).

People can have sex and enjoy each others' bodies in all sorts of ways. Certainly, if you consider the above list, you will notice that almost all of the body's openings can be used in sex. The vagina is the only opening that is part of the reproductive system, whereas the mouth and anus are the two ends of the digestive system. Thus, there are some people who believe that oral and anal sex are unnatural and they choose not to have sex in these ways. Other people have no problem with this. You have to decide for yourself what you think.

If you are absolutely sure that you are with a good man and that you love him or really like him, then it is up to you if you want to have sex with him or not, provided that both you and the man are over the 'age of consent' (see Chapter 10). If one or both of you is under the age of consent, then sex is against the law and you are not allowed to do it.

Penis-vaginal sexual intercourse

Penis-vaginal sexual intercourse is the 'normal version' of sex, which I did know at least something about.

Penis-vaginal sexual intercourse means the act in which a man's penis enters a girl/woman's vagina for the purposes of sexual pleasure or reproduction (having a baby).

Having sex may form or increase an emotional bond between the partners. Sexual arousal means your body getting stimulated, usually by touch, to get ready for sex. Sexual arousal of the man results in the erection of his penis. Sexual arousal of the woman results in natural lubrication of her vagina. To have sex, the erect penis is inserted into the vagina and one or both of the partners move their hips to move the penis backward and forward inside the vagina to cause friction. In this way, they stimulate themselves and each other, often continuing until one or both people has an orgasm.

The man having an orgasm causes semen to be ejaculated. If no contraceptive is used, the semen goes into the vagina. Sperm cells in the semen travel through the cervix, the uterus and into the Fallopian tubes. If a fertile egg is in a Fallopian tube, one of the sperm cells might manage to meet and fuse with this egg to make an embryo. If this happens, the embryo may move into the uterus and implant into its lining, which causes a pregnancy to begin.

People often have sex purely for pleasure, when they do not want to have a baby. For this, they use contraception. I will discuss contraception in more detail in Chapter 8. Sexually transmitted infections can be transmitted by penis-vaginal sex and there is a section on that in Chapter 8, too.

What they do not show on TV very well is that sex may be both sweaty and quite messy. Bodies can get sweaty when they get sexually aroused; and the production of both semen and vaginal lubrication can cause a certain amount of mess and stickiness. Some people are fine with this but others may choose to put a towel on the bed underneath, or change the bedding afterwards. It is a good plan to wash yourself, both before and after: after, because of it being sweaty and a bit messy;

before, because it is a matter of hygiene and it makes things much more pleasant for your partner if you smell nice and clean.

Sex is something that couples get better at with practice and the first time might not be altogether fun. Your first time ever might also be a bit painful, because your body will not be used to it. If you can relax, this might help (I know this from inserting tampons – if you are too tense or anxious, all the muscles around the vaginal passage tense up and you have no chance of getting anything in and any attempt hurts). Remember that, as Aspies, we tend to be more sensitive to certain sensory sensations and to pain than most people.

Also, there is a membrane-like tissue called the hymen that surrounds or partially covers the external vaginal opening. If your hymen is unbroken, penetrative sex for the first time might break it (which is perfectly normal and fine) but which might be a bit uncomfortable, or even painful, and you may bleed. People used to consider an unbroken hymen as proof that a girl was a virgin (which means someone who has never had sexual intercourse in their life). However, this is not right because your hymen could already be broken if you have ever used tampons. Also, playing some sports can cause your hymen to break; and some women are even born without a hymen.

I am not trying to worry you here or put you off by talking about possible pain or discomfort. I am just trying to say not to be surprised, panicked or alarmed if you have sex for the first time and find some of it to be a bit painful, because this would be perfectly normal. If you are in agony (which I think is unlikely unless you are in fact being attacked or abused), that is not normal and you should stop. Make a doctor's appointment and go and tell your doctor about this. If you are experiencing any amount of pain, tell your partner so he will know to be more gentle with you. If you want him to stop, tell him to stop. You are allowed to stop anything at any time for any reason. It is a good plan to stop if you are in a great deal of pain.

Other reasons that sex could be extremely painful include if you are too young to be having sex, or if you are being forced to have sex against your will (which is called rape). I will talk about these things in Chapters 10 and 12.

If the person you are with is not your boyfriend or husband, penis-vaginal sex is not ideal. If you have sex with someone who does not genuinely love you, you risk getting hurt emotionally and/

or physically. However, in the unlikely situation that someone is attacking you and you are in danger of being killed or injured if you do not do it, then your best option may be to do it and escape as soon as you can afterwards.

Okay, right then, deep breath and back to our explanation of the various types of sex…

Fingering

Fingering means the manipulation of the vulva or anus by a person's hand for a sexual purpose. The hand could be inside or outside the vulva or anus. If a finger goes into the vagina, this is called 'digital penetration of the vagina.' Fingering can be done by a man and a woman, by two women, or by two men (since the definition of fingering includes the anus). For the rest of this section, I am going to talk about fingering of the vulva.

Fingering is probably the most innocent version of sex, if it can be called that, but it is also the sneakiest because it can happen quite quickly and without your explicit permission if you are not prepared for it. So pay special attention to this next bit.

One thing a man might try to do is get inside your knickers. If his ultimate goal is to have sex with you (sooner or later), getting inside your knickers, and getting you prepared to allow this, is his step 1. One way of doing this, of course, is to remove your knickers, but another (far easier way) is to slide his hand into your knickers. This is the sneaky bit, because he can slide in his hand very quickly, whilst you are fully dressed and perhaps when you are not expecting it. In a non-abusive situation, this is likely to happen when you are kissing a boyfriend, typically whilst you are lying on a couch or a bed. In my opinion, it is also difficult to anticipate or realise what is about to happen, because if you are kissing him, you are going to be pretty distracted by that; also, you will not be able to see what he is doing or get any visual warning, because all you can see is his face (up so close that you cannot even focus on it and it is a sort of blur). Also, he may not stop kissing you to say: 'Excuse me, would you mind if I just put my finger into your vagina and moved it around a bit?'

So, it is highly likely that you will have no visual or verbal clues about what is going to happen. This only leaves the touch sense to alert you to what is going on, and no pre-warning. I have found this difficult, because I find touching and stroking to be generally a nice sensation. When I am enjoying a pleasant sensation, I am not naturally on my guard and thinking: 'Ooh this is something to be wary of.' I am feeling calm and relaxed and not in a state of high alert, watchfulness or anticipation, particularly if I am completely clueless as to what could happen next. Also, I have found that I am far less embarrassed by something when I cannot see what is happening. So, whereas my normal state of hyper-embarrassment would kick in if I could see what was going on, for some reason it does not, if I cannot see it.

So, given that there are no warnings by either sight or hearing, the only way you could know what is about to happen is by knowing what they are likely to do (which I am now going to tell you) and by using your touch sense to anticipate it.

So, right, the man has started to slide his hand in between your knickers and your body. If you do not do anything at this point, his next move will be to slide his hand against your vulva. At this point, he may massage your clitoris and/or insert his finger into your vagina, aiming to give you an orgasm. He may move his finger around inside your vagina. It might feel very nice. It is certainly invasive. It might feel scary, because it is an out-of-control experience. It might feel scary if it was something that you did not want to happen or did not know was going to happen.

Therefore, the knickers line is a very important boundary. Knickers are a very helpful bit of clothing here, because they define an obvious, physical boundary that you can both see and feel. This is helpful for those of us who get inconsistent body signals and who might not have a good overall awareness of where all our body parts are, especially when we are distracted or are under sensory overload.

If you *do* want fingering to happen, well, that is very easy because you do not need to do anything. But if you do *not* want to be 'fingered' in this way or by the particular person you are with, then you need to stop his hand from passing the knickers boundary. You do this by grabbing his wrist the instant his hand begins to go inside your knickers, and you pull his hand away. Your quick reaction is really important here because it will only take him a second or two to insert his finger into your vagina once he has passed the knickers boundary. Men understand that you pulling their hand away is a non-verbal way of you saying 'no'. In a non-abusive situation, the man will respect your 'no' here and stop, although he may try it again some other time and you will have to grab his wrist again if you still do not wish him to do this.

If the man refuses to stop when you ask him to or when you move his hand away, this is an abusive situation and you need to escape if this is at all possible.

If the man is not your boyfriend or husband, it is not advisable to allow him to finger you, and it is a good plan to say 'no' and to pull his hand away. However, if this does not work and he does it anyway, it is a sexual assault and this might be the first step on the path to you being raped by this man, sooner or later. In such cases, you probably would not be lying on a couch kissing him first, and the fingering could happen really at any time when you are alone, whether you are upright or lying down. Escape as soon as possible.

Oral sex

Confusingly, oral sex does not mean kissing, French kissing, or talking about sex. Oral sex is when you stimulate your partner's genitals with your mouth, lips or tongue (see NHS Choices 2010b). Oral sex can be performed on a man and on a woman. Oral sex on a man means your mouth around his penis or anus. Oral sex on a woman means his mouth around your vulva or anus. Oral sex can also be done between two men or two women.

If you are performing oral sex on a man's penis, his penis will become erect and he may well ejaculate. You can choose to pull your mouth away just before ejaculation, so that you do not take the semen into your mouth. Otherwise, you have two choices – to spit the semen out, or to swallow it. Semen has a very particular taste, which you may not like. It could make you choke, gag or feel sick – or you might be fine with it. The amount of semen that is ejaculated is around 5ml (the equivalent of a teaspoon).

You cannot get pregnant using oral sex alone, because even if you swallow some semen, it will then be in your digestive system, which is entirely separate from your reproductive system. However, you do need to be careful (if you do not want to get pregnant) that no semen is transferred indirectly (for example, on hands) to your vaginal area.

Sexually transmitted infections, including HIV, *can* be transmitted by oral sex, and any blood to blood contact increases the risk of this happening. Cold sores and gum abrasions are the most common ways for sexually transmitted infections to be transmitted during oral sex. Even small (microscopic) wounds, for example, a tiny scratch in your mouth, increase the risk of transmission. Such small wounds could be caused by brushing your teeth or eating crunchy foods beforehand. Using a condom can lessen the risk of transmission. There is also something called a dental dam, which is a small square of very thin rubber that is placed and held over the vulva or anus to provide a barrier between this and the other person's mouth to protect against sexually transmitted infections.

If the person you are with is not your boyfriend or husband, oral sex is not ideal, for the same reasons as given above for penis-vaginal sex.

If the person you are with is your boyfriend or husband, then it is up to you – just make sure this is really what you want, and not what you are being manipulated into. Some married people do oral sex and some do not. Some unmarried people do oral sex and some do not. There is no right or wrong answer: it is a matter of individual values and personal preferences.

A man might want you to give him oral sex because he wants something that feels like sex to him and stimulates his penis, but which will not get you pregnant and result in him becoming a father. It is also very intimate, and he may really enjoy the sensations.

If someone says oral sex does not count as real sex…well, you may choose not to believe that. It is intimate, and certainly is a form of sex, so, if you are wanting not to have sex before marriage or with someone you do not love, then oral sex may be something you choose to avoid.

If you do not want to do oral sex on someone else, or for oral sex to be done on you, be prepared to say 'no', make sure that you do say 'no', and then do not let yourself get talked into it.

Anal sex

Anal sex means inserting a penis (or another object) into the anus of a sexual partner, and can be done between a man and a woman, two men, or two women.

Usually, but not necessarily, when anal sex is between a man and a woman, this means his penis being inserted into your anus.

Some people find being on the receiving end of anal sex pleasurable because of the close proximity to sexual organs; some of the nerve endings for sexual stimulation are close by. Some people find being on the receiving end of anal sex painful, especially if they are anxious or stressed. Anxiety makes the muscles of the anus tense instead of relax, which causes pain and might lead to injury, such as a tear in the wall of the anus.

Anal sex has a low risk of pregnancy if done without vaginal sex, as the anus is part of the digestive, not reproductive, system, but there is still a risk because the vulva is close by and semen could inadvertently enter the vagina.

Many people think that you cannot get a sexually transmitted infection from anal sex, but this is not true. Anal sex has a higher risk of injury than vaginal sex, and a higher risk of transmission of sexually transmitted infections than many other types of sexual activity. The tissues of the anus and the rectum are thin, making them vulnerable to getting torn – in other words, an injury. Frequent anal sex is associated with medical problems such as haemorrhoids, anal prolapse, leakage, ano-rectal pain and ulcers and fissures (NHS Choices 2011a).

Ways to lessen the risks of pregnancy and sexually transmitted infections include to use a condom, and not to move immediately between anal sex and penis-vaginal sex without changing the condom. But watch out, as always, that you use the condom properly and that it does not break. It is also advisable to empty your bowels beforehand (have a poo) and to make sure the area is clean.

Reasons why a man might want to have anal sex with you include: their wanting something that feels like sex to them and stimulates their penis, but not wanting to get you pregnant or for them to become a father; because they might wrongly believe that there is no risk of infection transmission; and/or because they might get themselves more physical pleasure – the anus is usually tighter than the vagina, so it gives a firmer pressure on their penis, which they like.

If the person you are with is not your boyfriend or husband, anal sex is not advisable, for the same reasons as given above for penis-vaginal sex.

If the person you are with is your boyfriend or husband, then whether or not you have anal sex is up to you – just make sure this is really what you want, and not what you are being manipulated into.

Some married people do anal sex and some do not. Some unmarried people do anal sex and some do not. There is no right or wrong answer that everyone can agree on, since it is very much a matter of personal values and individual preference.

If you are sure you do want to have anal sex, then you should take precautions, use contraceptives and do more research on the subject than I have written here.

If you do not want to be the giver of anal sex to a man (i.e. you inserting some kind of object into his anus), then it is straightforward not to do it!

If you do not want to be the receiver of anal sex (i.e. you receiving a man's penis or another object into your anus), be prepared to say 'no' and make sure that you do say 'no'. If you do not want to have sex at all, then keep your knickers on, and anal sex is unlikely to happen.

If you are consenting to penis-vaginal sex but do not want anal sex, then ideally, if you have a good relationship with your partner, you will be able to communicate honestly with him and tell him, and he will respect your decision. I guess everything would be a bit simpler with more talking and communication. But sometimes things happen that are not verbally discussed and agreed first. The man often does not say: 'Now I would like to do such-and-such, is this okay?' In which case, you need to know your body (which is a good idea anyway). The vaginal opening is the one between your legs and the anus is the one a little further back, between your buttocks. If you feel anal penetration starting to happen, you will need to say 'no' and maybe also push your partner away to stop him.

CHAPTER 8

Safer Sex

What is safer sex?

If you do decide to have sex with someone, it is vitally important to be safe. 'Safe' in this context means:

- being with a good man, not being forced into having sex and not being attacked, beaten up, threatened, blackmailed, coerced or manipulated into it
- being protected from sexually transmitted infections
- not becoming pregnant if you do not want to and if you have not planned on having a baby.

'Safe' sounds like a very black and white term, but the truth is that there is never any total guarantee of safety for any of these three things. Sexual activity is not risk-free. You can never absolutely guarantee that any man is safe – there is always some element of trust, as each human being has their own free will which cannot be controlled by anyone else. A male condom can help protect you from sexually transmitted infections, but condoms can break and fail. Contraceptives help prevent an unwanted pregnancy, but no contraceptive is 100 per cent successful. Therefore, I would interpret 'safer sex' as 'making sex as safe as possible' rather than a 100 per cent guarantee of safety.

Let's consider these three points in turn:

Being with a good man

It can be very hard to tell a good man from a bad one. This is where your support network comes in. Get some opinions of people in your support network as to whether you are with a good man or not. This is something that you need to remember to communicate about. Even if your trusted person has not met your boyfriend, you can talk to them about him and what is happening in your relationship, and how he treats you, and they can tell you if he sounds nice or dodgy. Many non-spectrum people are good at this, so it is a good plan to pick a non-spectrum person from your support network.

Being protected from sexually transmitted infections

Sexually transmitted infections (STIs) are infections which could lead to diseases that have a significant probability of transmission by means of sexual behaviour, including penis-vaginal sex, oral sex and anal sex. It is not common for these to spread by fingering, but it is still possible (NHS Choices 2011a). To be on the safe side, it should be considered that all sexual activities that involve contact with the bodily fluids of another person have a risk of transmission of STIs. A person who has a sexually transmitted infection is not necessarily diseased themselves (yet), but could still transmit the infection to others. A person might have a sexually transmitted infection without their knowing it.

Ways of reducing the risk of transmission include vaccinations against some sexually transmitted infections, and using a male condom properly. With fingering, surgical gloves can be worn to reduce the risk (NHS Choices 2011a).

It is important to note that what protects you from getting pregnant accidentally is not necessarily the same thing as what protects you from sexually transmitted infections. In fact, the male condom is the only thing that does both jobs at once (NHS Choices 2011d). Therefore, even if you have chosen another type of contraceptive to use, such as the pill, you should also use a male condom to protect yourself from sexually transmitted infections. However, it is possible to make mistakes with using a condom, or to use it perfectly and for the condom to break anyway, so nothing is 100 per cent sure.

It is possible to get tested for sexually transmitted infections before starting a sexual relationship. If your sexual partner does not have a sexually transmitted infection, you will not be able to catch one from him.

If everyone only ever had sex with one partner in their life, then we would not have sexually transmitted infections in the first place. This is a good argument against having sex with lots of different people. Lots of people having sex with lots of other people is how these infections and diseases spread.

Information about sexually transmitted infections is available from the NHS website (NHS Choices 2011b) and by searching on Wikipedia; you do not need to remember this stuff in great detail, but it is a good idea to read it so that you are aware of what is out there.

The most basic knowledge you need is how to recognise an STI if you do become infected. Some common symptoms of STIs in a woman are:

- unusual discharge from the vagina (e.g. greenish, greyish or yellowish in colour; a strong, unpleasant, fishy odour)
- prolonged itchiness or general irritation around the genitals
- pain or discomfort when passing urine
- a sore, wart or blister on or around the genitals or anus
- pain during sexual intercourse
- pain in the lower abdomen.

It is very important to note that very often *there are no symptoms*, but the infection can still be damaging your body.

If you think you might have a sexually transmitted infection, the rule is that you have to get this checked out by your doctor. Some sexually transmitted infections are simple to treat if this is done promptly, but cause serious long-term health problems if left untreated. I would say the most serious sexually transmitted infection is probably HIV (the human immunodeficiency virus), which is a virus that weakens your ability to fight infections and cancer. AIDS (acquired immunodeficiency syndrome) is the final stage of HIV infection, when your body can no longer fight life-threatening infections. There is no cure for HIV, but there are treatments to extend quality and quantity of life (NHS Choices 2011b).

So, a sexually transmitted infection is absolutely *not* something to ignore if you feel a bit embarrassed, in the hope that it will go away. This is also not something to diagnose yourself – you need it properly diagnosed and treated by a doctor.

Not becoming pregnant if you do not want to – contraception

If you do not want to get pregnant, you need to use contraception. There is no pregnancy risk if the *only* thing you are doing is oral sex alone or fingering alone, but there is a risk of pregnancy with both penis-vaginal sex and anal sex. There is also some risk of catching sexually transmitted infections with both oral sex and fingering (NHS Choices 2011a).

There are currently around 15 different types of contraceptives, all with their own advantages and disadvantages. They are used in different ways and have different effects and possible side effects. Some contraceptives are suitable for some types of people but not others. Some protect against pregnancy in the short term and others over the long term. It is important to be aware that no contraceptive method is 100 per cent perfect. This means that even if you use contraception properly, there is a small chance that you will get pregnant anyway. Different contraceptives have different statistical likelihoods of success.

I found the following information on the UK's National Health website (NHS Choices 2011c), and this might be a good place to start your own research. This website has much more detailed information than I have written here, and if you look at it yourself, you can be sure of getting up-to-date information and that you get the complete information for your particular circumstances; also, please see your doctor to check your understanding. If you feel embarrassed, well, yes, I certainly know how you feel, but not getting pregnant unexpectedly is a lot more important than your embarrassment, so you need to be brave and discuss this with your doctor.

Some types of contraceptives include:

- *Barrier methods.* So called because they create a physical barrier which prevents sperm from reaching and fertilising an egg, so that an embryo/baby cannot be formed. Examples of these are the male condom (which fits snugly around an erect penis), the female condom (which sits in the vagina) and the diaphragm (which fits in the vagina, covering the cervix, and creates a seal against the vaginal walls). Male condoms are the only form of contraception that is proven to help prevent both pregnancy and sexually transmitted infections. Female condoms might or might not be effective against sexually transmitted infections – more research is needed.

- *Hormonal contraceptives.* Using a hormonal contraceptive means taking hormones into your body to temporarily interfere with your own hormones and your fertility. There is a great variety of hormonal contraceptives available and many different ways of delivering the hormones into your body. For example, you can either take a pill, have an implant put into your arm, have an injection, wear a patch, insert a vaginal ring or have an intrauterine system (IUS) fitted into your uterus. It is vital that you find out exactly when and how often you need to take the pill, fit the vaginal ring, have the injections or have the implant, patch or IUS replaced. Do *not* forget to do this. Use a diary or other organisational system to remind you. Some people believe that Aspies can be extra-sensitive to medications, and I would bear this in mind when considering any hormonal contraceptives. Also, your hormone balance is a delicate thing and you might want to consider whether you are okay with artificially interfering with this. Hormonal contraceptives do not protect you from sexually transmitted infections.

- *Intrauterine device (IUD).* Also known as the 'coil', this is an object placed in the uterus to prevent pregnancy. It releases copper, as opposed to hormones, in order to reduce the chances of pregnancy. An IUD does not protect you from sexually transmitted infections. Unlike some contraceptives that can be used by yourself and your partner alone, the intrauterine device (and the intrauterine system) needs to be fitted (and ultimately removed) by your doctor, and not by yourself. Fitting the IUD/IUS typically involves two internal examinations of your vagina/uterus by your doctor. The first internal examination is to assess if the IUD/IUS is suitable for you, and the second one is to actually fit the device. Having an internal examination involves taking off your knickers, lying on an examination couch, and a doctor inserting a small device called a speculum into your vagina. This holds open the vaginal walls so that the doctor can see and access your cervix and uterus. You might think I am stating the obvious here by saying you have to take off your knickers, and I suppose I am; but I did once attend an appointment to get assessed for contact lenses without any clue that the optician was going to touch my eyes! I found that deeply traumatic. I always find difficult experiences a bit easier if I am at least prepared for them and know what is going to happen. Having an internal examination might involve a lot of bravery on your part (it certainly would for me). If you want to do this, you may consider asking to have it done by a female doctor if this would make you feel safer and more comfortable.

- *Sterilisation.* Two further options, if you know absolutely for sure that you never want to have a baby, are female sterilisation and male sterilisation. These are surgical operations and they are permanent, so you should only do this if you are certain you will never change your mind and want to have a baby in the future. If you get sterilised, that should mean that you will never be able to have a baby, with any man. If a man gets sterilised, that should mean that he will never be able to get any woman pregnant. However, there is a very, very small chance that these operations will not work.

WHAT TO DO IF YOU REALISE THAT YOUR CONTRACEPTION HAS FAILED (OR IF YOU HAVE NOT USED ANY CONTRACEPTION)

First, I would really recommend that if you do not want to have a baby in nine months' time, you *always* use contraception. It is a really, really bad idea not to. But if you have not used it, for whatever reason, the following applies, just as it does for failures of contraception.

If you have not used contraception, or you realise that your contraception has failed (for example, you use a condom but afterwards, you notice that the condom has split), one option is to get an emergency contraceptive pill (also known as the 'morning-after pill') from a pharmacy or from your doctor. Emergency contraceptive pills are drugs intended to disrupt ovulation or fertilisation in order to prevent pregnancy. If you choose this option, take the pill as soon as possible. An alternative method of emergency contraception is to have an intrauterine device fitted as soon as possible.

It is better to act *right away* than to wait until it is too late and then have to consider an abortion.

Also, it would be a good idea to get tested for sexually transmitted infections. If you have one, this also needs to be treated sooner rather than later.

The male condom

I really do not want to get into the topic of contraceptives too deeply, because I am not suitably qualified, but using a male condom does seem extremely important because it is currently the best known way of giving dual protection against pregnancy and sexually transmitted infections. Also, using a male condom is quite a technical thing, and it is really important that you know how to do it properly and that you do it right. So, whilst I will not go into any further detail on other contraceptives, I do think it is important to talk a bit more about male condoms and how to use them. I researched this bit using the NHS website (NHS Choices 2011c; NHS Choices 2011e). I also found out later, by talking to a friend, that I had not understood it quite right, which also makes me think that my wordier form of explanation might be helpful to others.

The male condom is a form of barrier contraception. You can buy condoms at supermarkets, pharmacies, petrol stations and from vending machines in public toilets. You might also be able to get them free from your doctor or sexual health clinic in some countries.

Condoms are used during penis-vaginal sex, oral sex and anal sex. The condom should be put on before the penis comes into contact with your vagina, anus or mouth.

The male condom is a tubular shape which is closed at one end, in the same way that a sock is, but it is much smaller than a sock – this is just a shape comparison and nothing else. There is a teat at the closed end. Condoms are made from latex, which is a very thin, stretchy and flexible material. In use, the male condom fits snugly around the man's erect penis. The condom will stretch to do this – which means that one size of condom can fit different sizes of penis. In the packet, the tubular part is rolled up.

I am now going to describe how to use a condom. For ease of describing, I will talk in terms of 'you do this, you do that', but either the man or the woman can put the condom onto the man's penis.

1. First, you get the penis to be erect (probably very easy as it usually happens automatically when men are sexually aroused. Stimulating the penis by stroking or by oral sex, will probably cause it to become erect, too).

2. Hold the teat at the closed end of the condom between your finger and thumb, so that you squeeze the side walls of the teat together. This bit is really important. What you are aiming for is to minimise the amount of air trapped in the teat.

3. Place the teat (still squeezing this together) over the top of the erect penis. The base of the teat should be approximately level with the top of the penis. Do not pull the tip of the teat onto the top of the penis. There needs to be some length (about 1.5cm) between the top of the penis and the tip of the teat.

4. Keep holding the teat and unroll the tubular part of the condom down the length of the penis, so that the open end of the tube is at the base of the penis. The flexible, stretchy material of the condom ensures a snug fit which creates a seal around the penis. We now have a condom on the penis with effectively two closed ends.

5. Let go of the teat. Have a look at what you see. The condom should now be securely fitted around the penis, unable to slip up or down. You should see a gap between the tip of the teat and the top of the penis. The walls of the teat should still remain closed together, as you have effectively created a vacuum in the teat by squeezing the air out of it. It should look a bit like a balloon before it has been blown up.

6. If, instead, you see the teat looking more like a balloon that has already been blown up, full of air at the tip, then you have gone wrong. Alternatively, if instead you see that the tip of the teat is now sitting directly on top of the penis without any significant gap, you have also gone wrong. Take off the condom and start again with a new condom. Do not carry on with this condom, because it is not properly fitted and this is not safe.

7. If, and only if, the condom looks as described in step 5, then you can now have sexual intercourse. When the man ejaculates

semen from his penis, the semen is caught and kept between the penis and the condom, in the teat of the condom. The semen coming into the teat pushes the walls of the teat apart. If we are still thinking of the teat as being a bit like a balloon, the semen coming into the teat is like filling the balloon up with water. The semen cannot move into the annulus between the tubular part of the condom and the penis, because this annulus is sealed by the snug fit of the condom. The semen cannot escape out of either closed end of the condom, so it cannot enter directly into your vagina and fertilise an egg.

Now we can see the importance of allowing a gap between the top of the penis and the tip of the teat, and the importance of squeezing as much air out of the teat as possible. This provides the crucial space needed for the semen to go into. If you do not leave a gap, the semen has nowhere to go and the pressure of the semen acting on the end of the condom makes it much more likely that the condom will break. Also, even if you do leave a gap, but this gap is full of air (not a vacuum), we have a similar problem: the semen is coming out, but the space it is coming into is full of air and is therefore already pressurised. The semen therefore creates an additional pressure in this enclosed space, which acts on the condom and could cause it to break. This is a point that I never understood. I had heard of condoms possibly breaking but I thought that was because of possible failures of the material and/or workmanship. I did not realise this is also to do with how they are used or misused. It is mega-important to fit the condom correctly in the first place, because if it does break inside you, it is already too late in terms of safety, and you will not know it has broken (you will not feel it) until the penis is withdrawn and you can see the condom.

8. Shortly after ejaculation, the penis loses its erection and gets smaller and softer, whilst the condom remains in its stretched shape, which is still the size of the erect penis. Therefore, it is no longer a snug fit on the penis, leaving a gap in the annulus between the smaller, soft penis and the condom. The open end

of the condom is no longer sealed around the base of the penis, and there is a gap there too. We no longer have two closed ends of the condom. This means that there is a risk of the semen leaking down the outside of the penis and out of the open end of the condom, via this annular gap. If this were to happen when his penis is still in your vagina, the semen could enter directly into your vagina, and you could become pregnant.

9. Since this is exactly what you do not want to happen, the man should withdraw his penis from your vagina immediately after ejaculation, whilst it is still erect (so the condom is still a snug fit). As he does this, he should hold the condom at the base of the penis to maintain the seal and to make sure it does not come off.

10. Then, after withdrawal, you just remove the condom from the penis, being careful not to spill any semen, wrap it in tissue and put it in a bin.

The aim of the game here is that all the semen is caught within the condom and is trapped there until after his penis has left your vagina, so that all of it ends up in the bin, whilst none of it enters your vagina. After the condom has been disposed of, you still need to make sure that his penis does not come into contact with your vulva, since there may be traces of semen remaining on the penis.

Other important condom tips

- If you have sex again, use a new condom. Never reuse the same condom.

- If you are having sex for a long time, change the condom after every 30 minutes.

- Condoms do go out of date and might not work if they are too old, so always check the expiry date on the packet.

- Make sure you get a condom that has been properly approved by the appropriate regulator. In Europe, approved condoms carry the European CE mark.

- Store condoms in a cool, dry place. Do not use lotions or oils with a condom, as these can weaken it.

- Do not use both a male condom and a female condom at the same time, because friction between these two condoms could cause either or both to slip out of the correct place, or tear.

- Do not use two male condoms at the same time, for the same reason.

Possible objections to using a condom

To use a male condom as a contraceptive requires the man to agree and co-operate in using it (in contrast to a contraceptive pill, for example, which does not). Since condoms are so fantastic with the dual benefits of preventing pregnancy and STIs, I think that all decent men should agree to use one unless there is a very good reason against it (for example, an allergy to the condom material – in which case, you need to find an alternative solution). However, be aware that some people do not like using condoms and some men will object to using one. For example, they might find it awkward to stop and put the condom on, or they might object that it diminishes the sensations of having sex.

Neither of these are valid reasons not to use a condom, in the light of the much more important advantages of using one, and could be considered as very selfish. Thus, I suggest that you should be very wary of getting talked out of using a condom just because of one of these reasons. This is another thing to be assertive about: say what you want, and then be very careful about possibly getting talked into changing your mind, being manipulated or coerced into not using a condom and having risky, unsafe sex instead. Some sexually transmitted infections will make you ill and some are life-threatening, for example HIV which can develop into AIDS. Remember that your life is at stake here. Unprotected sex is not something that it is okay to go along with if you find it difficult to say 'no'. These are the facts and beware of anyone lying to you and telling you otherwise.

CHAPTER 9

Pregnancy and Abortion

Pregnancy

Most people get pregnant because they want to have a baby and because they planned it. They deliberately have penis-vaginal sex, without using contraception, with someone they love (and may be married to) because they want to have a baby. Sperm from the man fertilises an egg inside the woman, these fuse together and a foetus (an unborn baby) is formed.

But sometimes people get pregnant when they do not want to. You can get pregnant if you have sex:

- without using contraception
- with contraception and the contraception fails
- only once
- when you are still a child (eight-year-olds have given birth)
- with your boyfriend/partner/husband
- with a friend or a stranger
- with someone you do not want to have sex with
- with someone who forces you to have sex with them
- with someone who is in your family (for example, your father, step-father or older brother). Having sex with a close family member such as these is called incest and is illegal in many countries. Family members who are genetically related share a lot of common genes and incest is potentially bad for any resulting baby, as they may get two copies of the same gene.

This can cause serious health problems for the baby – for example, disabilities or deformities.

Basically, if you have sex, no matter who it is with, legal or illegal, whether or not you are in love, whether or not you meant to have sex or wanted to, and whether or not you intended to get pregnant, there is always a chance you *will* get pregnant. Your body will not be able to distinguish who you are having sex with and why, and your body will always do its best to start a baby.

If you get pregnant because you wanted to, fantastic – congratulations! Be sure to visit your doctor so that they can look after you and so that you can learn what to do to have a healthy pregnancy.

If you get pregnant but you did not want to, you have the following options:

- have the baby and keep it, even though you did not plan this
- have the baby and give it up for adoption after it is born
- have an abortion in the early stages of pregnancy to kill the foetus and to stop the pregnancy.

Abortion

Abortion is not contraception. It is the termination of a pregnancy by the removal from the uterus of the foetus (unborn baby). Because this does, in the eyes of some people, amount to the killing of an unborn baby, not everyone agrees with it. Have a think about whether this is something you would be prepared to do, morally.

If you do become pregnant and decide to have an abortion, sooner is much, much better than later. This is because at the very start of a pregnancy, the foetus is little more than a bundle of cells, but near the end, it is more like a fully developed baby. In fact, the foetus very quickly becomes something recognisable as a tiny forming baby and not a bundle of cells. You may feel that if you are going to kill something, it would be far better to kill a bundle of cells, in which case, you need to act as soon as possible. There is an upper limit to when an abortion can be performed. Once the foetus has developed to the point where it could survive if it were born prematurely (this is known as 'viability'), abortion is not legal. The stage of pregnancy at which this is considered to be the case varies slightly from one country to another, but is generally around five to six months.

Abortion is not risk-free (neither is pregnancy), but it is both safer and less traumatic for you if you are early on in the pregnancy. This is really important, so speed is of the essence. Do not spend months trying to decide what to do. Do not fail to do anything because you feel embarrassed about talking to anyone. Do not fail to do anything because you are confused and you hope that the problem will go away. It will not. Do talk to your doctor and your safe people. Abortion is not an easy option. Mothers feel sad and grieve when they lose their babies. You might feel sad and grieve if you lose your unborn baby. Pregnancy causes a lot of hormonal changes, and so does stopping being pregnant; these hormonal changes will also affect your emotions.

If you do become pregnant unintentionally, and cannot decide what to do, it is very important to seek unbiased, professional counselling as soon as you can. The best outcome for any woman is when she can make an informed, well-considered choice for herself, whether it is to have an abortion or to proceed with the pregnancy.

If you do not want to have an abortion but neither do you want to take care of a child, having the baby and giving it up for adoption is an alternative option.

Please see the Resources section at the end of the book for contact details of agencies who can offer information and advice about pregnancy, abortion and adoption.

CHAPTER 10

Too Young for Sex?

What is the 'age of consent'?

The 'age of consent' is a legal term which means the age at which someone can legally consent to sexual activity. Sexual activity without consent, regardless of age, is a criminal offence in many countries. The age of consent differs from country to country, and some countries do not have an age of consent.

In the UK, the age of consent is currently 16 – this is true for England, Wales, Scotland and Northern Ireland. However, if the other person is in a position of trust over you (for example, a teacher, coach or care worker), the age of consent is then 18 instead (NSPCC factsheet 2012).

For the USA, there are different laws in each US state, but the age of consent in all states is currently between 16 and 18 years old.

In Canada, the age of consent is 16 for penis-vaginal sex and oral sex, and 18 for anal sex. The age of consent is also 18 for sexual exploitation, which means prostitution and pornography, or when it occurs in a relationship of authority, trust or dependence (for example, with a teacher, coach or babysitter) (Canada Online 2012; Department of Justice 2011).

In Australia, the age of consent also differs between different states. The age of consent is 16 in the Australian Capital Territory, New South Wales, Northern Territory, Victoria and Western Australia. The age of consent is 17 in Tasmania and South Australia. In Queensland, the age of consent is 16 for oral sex and penis-vaginal sex, but 18 for anal sex (Australian Institute of Family Studies 2012).

Please note, this is the best information I have been able to find out as I am writing it, but I am not a legal expert, just a person looking up the information. The age of consent is defined in laws, which can and do change over time as new laws are passed. Also, the age of consent is surprisingly complicated in many countries, beyond the level of detail I have given here, as there is often additional information for particular circumstances (for example, for two consenting 15-year-olds). So, if you are a young person, it is a good idea to find out for yourself what the age of consent is in your country. This is easy to do: use the internet, go to www.google.com and type 'age of consent' and the name of the country and/or state that you are in. It is a good idea to check out at least three different sources of this information to make sure that they agree, because not everything that you find on the internet is accurate. If you find a government website, that might be best.

The age of consent is important (and hence a matter of law) because it aims to safeguard young people. The law sees people who are younger than the age of consent as not being legally competent to make their own decisions about sex, because children and young people can be easily tricked and manipulated into thinking they want something that they do not, or into behaving in a way that other people want them to (rather like Aspies of all ages, actually). For example, in the UK, since the age of consent is 16 years old this means that 16 is considered to be 'adult', whereas 15 or younger is 'child', as far as being able to give genuine, true consent to sex is concerned.

Having sex when you are too young

Sex is an activity for adults. Sex is not intended for children, young teenagers, or anyone who has not yet reached puberty. Having sex when you are too young might be very painful, because your body is not ready for it.

However, some children and young people do have sex or do other sexual activities. Some of these young people freely choose to do it, but some of them get forced to do it even though they do not want to, which is one of the most horrific things that I know about.

Any man (or boy) having sex with a girl who is below the age of consent is committing child abuse and is guilty of rape or sexual assault, no matter who the man is, what the reason, and no matter whether the girl has agreed to it or not. Some types of sexual activity constitute a sexual assault even if they do not fall into the definition of rape (a legal definition which varies between countries, but generally means being forced to have sex with someone).

What if this is happening to you?

If any of this, or anything similar to this, has happened to you in the past, or is currently happening to you, I am very sorry, this was very wrong of the other person and is not your fault. My heart is breaking for you. If you have not ever told anyone about this, you must tell one of your safe adults and they can get you some help and keep you safe. If the sex or rape is still happening repeatedly to you, we need to get this to stop and we can do this, but only if you tell someone. You might not feel that you want to tell anyone what is happening to you or that you are able to tell. You might feel embarrassed, ashamed and frightened, and all these are very normal feelings which anyone would feel in the circumstances. You have nothing to be ashamed about, however, as, whatever the circumstances, you have done nothing wrong and you are not guilty. When children are sexually abused, that is never, ever their fault. Whatever you might be feeling, it is incredibly important that you do tell someone, and the sooner you do this, the sooner you will be safe. Aspies are very brave and you can be brave about this. Other people will admire you for being so brave. It may be an incredibly difficult thing to do but it will make your life so much better in the long run.

If you are not sure whether what is happening to you is okay or not, then you still need to tell someone, to be on the safe side.

Examples of the types of people who you might choose to tell, if appropriate, include your mother, your father, your older, grown-up sister, your aunt, your school teacher, a member of the police, a social worker, an autism support worker, your doctor or an adult in your church or other community. Some of these types of people will not be allowed to keep secret what you tell them, but that is a very good thing and is to ensure your protection. This is not to say that all the specific people in these roles in your life are necessarily good choices – you need to judge who you can trust and who you cannot. You should pick someone who you can be sure will put your best interests as a higher priority than the interests of the man who is abusing you.

You need to pick someone who is not afraid of, or in the power of, your abuser.

More information on what to do is in Chapter 12.

CHAPTER 11

Making Your Choices
and Acting on Them

The first thing to realise is that, because your body is within your boundaries, what happens and does not happen to your body is your choice. This applies to any kind of touching, kissing and sex.

Often, when I have made the wrong choice in my life, it is because I have failed to realise that there is a choice to make. If we do not actively choose, sometimes other people will choose for us.

Do you want to have sex?

If you are absolutely sure that you are with a good man and that you love him or really like him, then it is up to you if you want to have sex with him or not, provided that both you and the man are over the age of consent (see Chapter 10).

However, make sure that if you are agreeing to have sex, that you are really sure about doing this, and that this is what you freely agree to. Freely agreeing means not being forced into it by someone else's manipulative or aggressive behaviour, and doing it because you truly want to and not because you are afraid of the consequences of not doing it. An example of manipulative behaviour is someone threatening you or someone trying to take away your choice or make you feel guilty if you do not do what they want. An example of aggressive behaviour is someone being violent to you or shouting at you to get you to do what they want. Sex is risky because some types of sex might result in an unwanted pregnancy and some types might result in you getting a sexually transmitted infection (see Chapter 8). Also, sex with the right person for the right reasons can help you emotionally, but sex with the wrong person or for the wrong reasons can harm you emotionally. So, you need to be very sure that you really want to do it.

This is something to think about first and decide if you would want to do it or not. Be sure to make up your own mind. Do not let someone talk or coerce you into having sex if you do not want to do it. Anyone telling you that you *do* want to do it should be treated with the greatest suspicion. How could they know what you want? Such a person is actually manipulating you, trying to get you to believe that you do want it, when you may not.

Do not have sex with anyone just because they threaten to leave you if you do not, or because you are scared they will leave you if you do not. Anyone threatening to leave you if you do not have sex with them is a horrible person and you should leave them in any case.

Do not have sex just because everyone else seems to be doing it. Actually, quite a lot of people are *not* doing it, too. Do not have sex with someone only because they expect you to do it. Only do it if you are completely sure that *you* want to. Some people believe that you should not have sex before being married to the person. Think about whether you agree with this or not. If you do agree that this is right, then you should not have sex before you are married.

I would advise that you do not have sex with, or be the girlfriend of, anyone who is horrible to you and who does not love and cherish you. This means no liars, no users, no abusers, no violent people, no aggressive people or manipulators, no-one who puts you down and no-one who does any nasty behaviour to you on purpose. If you find yourself thinking anything along the lines of: 'I will go out with this person who treats me badly because no-one else would ever want me,' then this is a very bad reason to go out with them. You do not know for sure that no-one else would ever want you. This kind of thought is a signal that you need to work on your self-esteem. Go see your support people and your friends, find out why they love you, write it down and look at it every day. Also make sure to read Chapter 3 of this book.

It is my feeling that if you are with someone you do not love and who you are not emotionally close to, the physical sensations that happen as a result of sexual activities are really pretty meaningless. It seems wrong, perhaps because the physical closeness is not matching the lack of emotional closeness, and the inconsistency here feels to me like a sort of lie. I thought in the past that perhaps by being physically close to someone, I might become emotionally close to them, but my experience is that this is not how it works. Emotional closeness follows from trust, openness, honesty and genuinely knowing and liking the other person's soul, and cannot be gained by physical acts if these other things are not there.

How do you stop men doing things you do not want them to do?

Okay, the first thing is to decide where your limits are: where is and is not safe touch for you on your body and what you are prepared to allow.

To summarise a bit, if the person is not your boyfriend, then touch in any of the sexual regions is not okay, under almost any circumstances. I suppose there will always be exceptions, like someone having to do heart massage on you to save your life, but almost always, they are not allowed to touch your breasts, chest, thighs, vulva or bottom, either through or underneath your clothing or without your clothes on. This is true no matter who the person is, how they describe what they are doing, for example, 'massage', rather than 'sex act', how much you trust them, or even if they tell you that it is okay (this is a lie), or that you want it to happen (this is them manipulating you).

If the person is your boyfriend, you have to work out where your limits are and what you are willing to do and not do, before you get into a tricky situation. In tricky situations, if we have not thought it out first, our default position is normally to be passive, which allows the man to do exactly what he wants to us, whether we like it or not.

If your boyfriend is touching you, remember where your limits are. If his hand starts to go beyond these limits (which it might well do), as soon as this happens, pick it up by his wrist and move it away. If he does not stop, then do this again, more forcefully. You can also say: 'No, I do not want you to do that.' Speak clearly, confidently and firmly – not a meek whisper. If your boyfriend is decent, then he will stop and respect your boundaries.

If any man refuses to stop when you ask him to or when you move his hand away, this is an abusive situation and you need to escape if this is at all possible. It is always dangerous to be with a man who does not respect your 'no' when it comes to sexual acts. If he does not stop, then this is a big warning sign that you have to get away right now because you could get raped. If he does not respect the smaller boundaries, he might not stop at the largest one of all.

In this case, here are some options:

- Run away.

- Scream (this distracts him and hopefully attracts the attention of any people nearby).

- Set off a rape alarm. You can buy these and carry one in your pocket – the noise will give you sensory overload, but it will also give him sensory overload and it is a good way to attract attention and to scare him off. But if you are so sensitive to noise that setting off the alarm might make you unable to see, move or know where your legs are, then setting off a rape alarm might not be a good plan.

- Hitting, biting, kicking and punching are all morally fine options in this situation. However, if you do this but are then unable to run away, remember he might hit you back and he is likely to be stronger than you.

If the man is not your boyfriend, any type of sex is not allowed to happen and is, thankfully, extremely unlikely to happen. Almost always, not having sex with someone is your choice to make, and if you say 'no', verbally or non-verbally, then sex will not happen. In a very extreme and abusive situation though, a man might force you to have sex with him. This is called either rape or sexual assault, depending on which type of sex it is and the country you are in.

The personal safety rule

Throughout our lives, we are given a lot of rules for many different reasons. Some rules are there to protect us. Other rules are there to protect other people, animals or the environment.

Some rules are society rules of social interaction – rules of polite behaviour that most people know and that generally make people feel comfortable if they are followed. I will call these 'politeness rules'.

Here are some *politeness* rules:

- Be a good girl.
- Be polite.
- Do not hit people, bite them or kick them.
- Do not argue.
- Do what you are told.
- Do not scream at people.
- Do what authority figures tell you to.
- Meet the social expectations of whoever you are with.
- Do not lie.
- Keep your promises.
- Keep other people's secrets.

However, the *personal safety* rule is:

- Do whatever you need to do to be safe. If you are not being threatened, say 'no' in whatever way you can to protect your boundaries. If you are being threatened but you can escape, do so, even if that involves breaking any or all of the politeness rules. If your life is in danger and there is no reasonable means of escape, then do whatever the person asks of you, even if you get raped, until an escape opportunity arises, at which point you escape using absolutely any tactics possible, however many other rules you may need to break.

Some rules are more important than others. There are some situations in life where you cannot keep one rule without breaking another. It is at these times when it is crucial to know which rule is the most important.

The personal safety rule is much more important than all of the politeness rules put together. This means that you are allowed to break all of the politeness rules if you need to, in order to keep the personal safety rule.

Although I have written a lot about saying 'no' to things that are not allowed, you should disregard this in the awful (and very unlikely) situation that someone is threatening your life. I am sorry to have to include this, but if this ever happens and escape is not possible, you should comply with your attacker to save your life. The number one rule is stay alive. Being raped is bad but being dead is worse. If you comply with your attacker to keep yourself alive, you can get help and healing afterwards. No worrying, no guilt, the rule is that you do whatever you have to do to stay alive. Every bit of emotional damage and most physical damage is fixable later if you stay alive.

If you do get raped or sexually assaulted, or have any near misses, you need to tell someone and get help. If this has happened to you in the past, whether you were a child at the time, a teenager or an adult, and whether it happened recently or many years ago, once or many times, I am so very sorry for your suffering. You need to tell someone about this and get help too. Chapter 12 is about rape and sexual assault and has further information. Also, after getting out of any immediate danger you may still be in from the person who abused you, you might need some emotional healing, which is discussed in Chapter 13.

What to Do if You Get Raped

I have written this book to try to give you some of the knowledge and 'rules', some of which I did not have, in order that, all being well, you can be safe and have good experiences. Unfortunately, it is not always possible to stop something really bad happening, even if we know all the rules and even if we act perfectly, sensibly, intelligently and with great skill. Most men are stronger than us and can overpower us and, although most men are nice, a very small number of them are very bad indeed. Sometimes, even with the best precautions, women and girls are just unlucky. If you are very unfortunate, you can get raped or sexually assaulted. Rape has a slightly different definition in different countries, but generally means someone having sex with you without your having agreed to it. Other acts may be sexual assaults, even if they do not fall into the precise definition of rape. In this section, I will talk about 'rape' but a lot of this is applicable to other sexual assaults too.

I based the following on information that I found on the Rape Crisis Centre Glasgow website (undated) and I have also expanded on this information.

What to do if you have just been raped

1. ESCAPE

Get as far away as you can from the person who raped you. Get to a safe place where he cannot come after you.

2. CALL FOR HELP

If you are in any danger, phone the police immediately. Make sure that you know the emergency number for the police in your country. In the UK, the phone number is 999; in the US, it is 911. Tell the police what happened, who did it and where they and you are now.

3. GET SUPPORT

Tell someone in your support network, so that they can come and be with you and help you feel and be safe. A rape is a very awful thing and you are likely to feel some, or all, of the following: scared, tearful, stressed, anxious, victimised, disgusted, violated, dirty, angry and unsafe. Having someone from your support network with you could help you to stabilise some of these emotions. Tell them *immediately*. Do not worry about bothering them or that they might be busy. Right now, your needs are more important.

4. NO WASHING

Do not wash yourself, take a shower or throw away any of your clothing (yet). You might really want to do these things because being raped can make you feel dirty. But this is not a good plan because it destroys evidence which could be used against your attacker.

5. CHECK FOR BLEEDING

Check if you are bleeding (whether or not you feel any pain). Check especially around the area of your vulva and anus.

6. NEED FOR HOSPITAL?

If you are bleeding, if you have bumped your head or if you were unconscious for any time, go to the Accident and Emergency section of the nearest hospital immediately. You might want to ask a person in your support network to go with you. This is a good idea because of the very stressful and awful experience you have just had, and because of the bad things you are likely to be feeling. You do not have to do this on your own. The way to not be on your own is to ask for support.

7. EMERGENCY CONTRACEPTION

Get and take some emergency contraception (for example, the emergency contraceptive pill – also known as the 'morning-after pill') from your doctor, a hospital or a pharmacy. This should be done as soon as possible but certainly within 72 hours of the attack.

8. MAKE A PLAN AND TAKE STEPS TO STOP IT HAPPENING AGAIN

This means you need to tell someone what has happened and get help for how to be safe in the future from the person who raped or sexually abused you. You may decide (now or in the future) to report the person to the police, but in the meantime, you need to keep yourself safe.

Who you pick to tell is important here. They must be intelligent and a very good, moral person. This could be the person you contacted in step 3 or someone else. You need to pick someone who you can be sure will put your best interests as a higher priority than the interests of the man who abused you, and someone who is not afraid of, or in the power of, your abuser. Think hard and choose the person you trust the most. All being well, this person will help you and the abuse will never happen again. However, if they do not believe you or if they do not do anything to help, then you need to find the person you trust the second-most and tell them. If this does not work, you find the person you trust the third-most and tell them, and so on, until you are safe. How you tell your trusted person does not matter. If it is too hard to tell them by speaking, you can write down what happened to you on a piece of paper and give it to them, or send them a letter or e-mail. You do not need to use eye contact or say any words out loud. Another good option is to go directly to the police or social services.

There is hope and there is a way to be safe. You absolutely do not give up communicating until you are safe. You do not give in to any threats that your abuser might have made against you telling anyone, because your abuser's biggest weapon is your silence, and his threats are probably unrealistic – this is him trying to manipulate you because he does not want to go to prison. Examples of threats not to believe include:

- 'If you tell anyone, I will kill you.'

- 'If you tell anyone, I will kill someone you love.'

It is not easy, risk-free or consequence-free to kill anyone. It would not be in your rapist's best interests to either murder you or anyone else, because he would be likely to go to prison for murder (which carries a harsher sentence than rape) and he would not want that. This is the person trying to scare you into silence. This should not be possible if you escape and then immediately tell the police, who can then act to protect you and anyone else who was threatened.

- 'If you tell anyone, someone you love will be so upset they will have a heart attack.'

People almost never have heart attacks just because they hear some upsetting news, and getting you safe is the most important thing here, all risks considered.

Of course, I cannot say these things with 100 per cent certainty as everyone has free will, but I do think there is a very, very, very great likelihood of these being empty threats (lies) and threats you can safeguard from by going to the police. The motivation of your rapist is to make you so scared that you never say anything to anyone. But not telling anyone means that you are protecting your rapist, and not protecting yourself or those you love.

These kinds of threats can be the reason that some people never tell about their rape, or do not tell for years afterwards. But telling is almost certainly the right thing to do, and the sooner the better.

Instead of giving into any threats, pretend that you are not going to tell anyone when/if you are with him (practise your lying skills – it is okay to lie in this situation), but as soon as you can, get away, tell someone, get safe, and then never go back to the abuser, ever again. It may be very hard to talk about what has happened (or is happening) to you. You might feel very scared. But it is important to tell someone, even if you are really scared, because the most important thing is that you get help. Do not give in to the fear.

There is also the choice to call a telephone helpline. For example, in the UK, if you are a child, you could telephone Childline on 0800 1111. If you are in another country, or if you are not a child, you could go onto the internet, go to www.google.com and then type 'sexual abuse helpline' into the search bar. Alternatively, autism charities often have telephone helplines and you could telephone one of them. Again, use the internet to find the phone number – for example, type 'autism charity helpline' into the search bar. If you do not feel able to, or wish to, use the telephone, you may be able to write an e-mail to the organisation instead.

These next two steps (9 and 10) are optional and brave. But I would do them if I were you, and I know that you are brave because Aspies have a lot of courage.

9. GO TO YOUR LOCAL RAPE CRISIS CENTRE OR SEXUAL ASSAULT REFERRAL CENTRE

Telephone your local Rape Crisis Centre or Sexual Assault Referral Centre. You will be able to find their contact details on the internet – go to Google and type in these words and the place where you live. Since you should not wash or shower before you do this step, you should do this as soon as possible after steps 1 to 8 above. Also, the sooner you do it, the more likely it is that the evidence will be preserved.

The centre will give you an appointment and you will go and see them. You will be seen by a female doctor and nurse who will ask you questions and examine your body. You will have to take off your knickers, as they will need to examine the area underneath your knickers. They will need to give you an internal examination, which means you lying on an examination couch and them putting a small device called a speculum into your vagina so they can see and access your cervix and uterus. They may also need to touch and examine your anus. You will need to be very brave and allow them to do this. They will be kind and as gentle as possible. They will be very nice and comforting and they will make you feel safe. They will reassure you that what has happened is not your fault. As they examine your body, they will get, record and store evidence which will confirm that you are telling the truth.

Going through this procedure might feel very scary and embarrassing, because having an intimate internal examination is an unusual thing to do. But it is completely safe. The doctor and nurse are working to protect you and not abuse you, and it is okay to trust them. The examination might feel a bit funny, but it should not be horrendously painful, and they will probably tell you what they are going to do before they do it, so you have a warning. You could explain to them that you are an Aspie and that you need them to be very clear with their explanations and very, very gentle with you.

The good thing about doing this step is that you might not yet have decided if you want to report the rape to the police. If you do this step, the evidence is then collected, everything urgent is taken care of, and you can take your time about deciding if and when to go to the police (optional step 10 below). If there is not a Rape Crisis Centre where you live, you can go to your local police station and they should be able to organise the same thing for you from there. Since I got this information from the Rape Crisis Centre Glasgow website, other centres might do things slightly differently and not exactly as I have written here, but the procedure is likely to be very similar.

10. TELL THE POLICE

Optional step 10 is to tell the police about your rape. This is a brave thing to do because it may result in you having to go to court and answer questions about it. This is a morally good thing to do because the police may be able to arrest the person who did it, punish him, and stop him from going on to rape other people. If you disclose that you are an Aspie, you may be able to get the court to treat you especially kindly (Aspies count as vulnerable people) and the court may let you give evidence via a video link or from behind a screen, so that it is less scary for you.

You can ask someone in your support network to come with you to the police station. If you have to go to court, I would definitely ask someone in your support network to go with you. I had to go to court once and it did not occur to me to ask someone to go with me. I was very scared and completely panicked and it would have been much easier if I had had someone with me to calm me down. If you have already done step 9, reporting the rape to the police is not urgent, except that it is still good to do it as soon as you feel able, in order to protect yourself and other women and girls from the person who raped you. Your rape is not likely to be an isolated incident, and if the person did that to you, he will also try to do it to others. Reporting the rape is therefore an act of love and protection on your part towards other women and girls.

11. SEE YOUR DOCTOR

See your doctor and ask to be tested for sexually transmitted infections.

12. GET SOME EMOTIONAL HEALING

If you were unlucky enough to get raped, I am so very sorry. A rape or other sexual assault can make you feel very bad – it is one type of emotional wound. When people are wounded physically, their wounds often heal automatically over time. When people are wounded emotionally, complete healing does not happen automatically and it is a good idea to get some emotional healing. You can read about emotional healing in Chapter 13.

PART 3

Emotional Healing

CHAPTER 13

Emotional Healing

If you have ever had any dodgy experiences with a man who was not your boyfriend or any sexual experiences that you did not want but could not stop, these can hurt you badly, emotionally. This is the case whether you got raped or whether what happened to you was far less than an actual rape. This is true for everyone, but possibly particularly true for Aspies because we are extra-sensitive to pretty much everything: sensory stimulus, emotions, praise, criticism, medicines, food, the environment, etc. You name it, and we are more sensitive to it! I seem to be extra-sensitive to everything except what other people are thinking and feeling…

A dodgy experience with a man happened to me, and I did not know what to do about it. I told a friend at the time, but we then went on with our lives and I never dealt with it properly. My mind suppressed it and I quite literally forgot all about it for 14 years. But part of my subconscious did not forget about it because I never dealt with it. Suppressing it probably protected me for a while, but it is not a permanent solution. Whatever you try to push to the back of your mind will some time pop back up to the front. All that happens is the back of your mind becomes very crowded and you have no control over when the horrors resurface. Even if you cannot consciously remember it anymore, your subconscious still knows about it and will use it to create all sorts of fears and behaviours in your life that you probably will not understand.

Other possible effects of an unwanted sexual experience include depression, shame, guilt, panic attacks, eating difficulties, relationship problems, sleeping difficulties, substance abuse, fear, anger, flashbacks and self-harming (Rape Crisis Scotland 2010). You may experience one, lots or none of these. I am not writing this to scare you, but to make you aware. These effects are a very good reason to get emotional healing.

The good news is that emotional healing is possible, even for very deep emotional wounds. There is a way, and you can do it.

There are five parts to emotional healing:

1. Tell a safe person what happened to you, so you are not trapped in your own private horror about it.

2. Either with your safe person or alone, work through any feelings you may have of embarrassment, fear, anxiety, guilt and shame. Make sure you are not blaming yourself for things that were not your fault. I find it really helps to do this with someone else, because they are likely to see the situation more clearly and objectively than me.

3. Forgive yourself for anything you feel you did that contributed to any part of the situation.

4. Be angry!

5. Forgive the other person (but do not forget).

Let's look at these in turn.

1. Tell a safe person what happened to you

Yes, I know it is hugely embarrassing to talk about any of this stuff, and bad sexual experiences are something that women and girls often feel too embarrassed and scared to admit. But keeping secret something that is really bad keeps all the hurt locked up inside you, with nowhere to go, which is not good for you. I have found that things seem a lot worse when they are bouncing around my head than when I manage to tell someone else.

How you tell them does not matter. If it is too hard to tell them by speaking, you can write down what happened to you on a piece of paper and give the paper to your trusted person, or send them a letter or e-mail. You do not need to use eye contact or say any words out loud.

I am not sure that the words 'embarrassed' and 'scared' can ever really get across the intensity of feeling that is experienced. When faced with having to tell my safe person what had happened to me, I was a shaking, sweaty mess – absolutely terrified – and I was struggling to speak, although I was in no danger and was talking about something that had happened many years ago. How I told my safe person was from somewhere within the depths of an enormous hug, in which I was wrapped up and held tenderly like a child. I felt entirely surrounded and protected, safe and warm and comfortable, and the rest of the world melted away. Whilst I was speaking, I could not do eye contact but I knew that my safe person was accepting me and not rejecting me because she kept holding me and did not push me away. When she spoke, all I could hear was her gentle voice in my ear, which quietened my thoughts and my fears. I was extraordinarily lucky to get to do it like this.

My safe person spoke out forgiveness for me and the other person involved, told me that I was not guilty, just innocent and with a childlike heart, which is a very lovely thing to have, but which also means that I can be so easily taken advantage of. I confessed some things that I felt ashamed of and very scared to admit to, but she did not say anything critical or judgemental to me and continued being comforting and compassionate. She said what had happened to me was classic, someone preying on the innocent, and that even if I did not fully understand it was wrong, the other person certainly did. She said the uncleanness is gone and that the chain between me and the other person is broken and that I am free. This oh-so-tenderly and safely pieced my shattered soul back together. I did not know it straight away, because I was exhausted and overwhelmed, but about six hours later I felt fantastic and I really did feel free and that it was all sorted out. Telling her was so hard to do, but I received the most enormous gift through doing it.

I think there is something about telling what has happened to someone you really trust and who is going to help you feel better that breaks the power of the thing that has hurt you. It ends up feeling a whole lot less shameful. Things like rape and sexual abuse are not talked about very much, but they are actually happening to lots of people all the time. So, if this has happened to you, you are not alone and there is nothing wrong with you or dirty about you because it happened. But if you do not tell anyone, then no-one can help you. Just do it. I know that you can.

The safe person I chose was someone I already knew from my support network, who was not acting in a professional capacity.

However, your choice of safe person is entirely up to you. If you do not want to tell anyone you know, another choice is to find an experienced professional who can offer counselling and support. Please see the Resources section at the end of the book for contact details of agencies who can offer help and advice.

2. Work through any feelings you may have of embarrassment, fear, anxiety, guilt and shame

I figured out that my best hope of getting any emotional healing was to talk about my experiences with one of my safe people. I was having some really strong emotions about what had happened, and I could not sort them out on my own. I needed help. But ironically, although I needed help to sort out my feelings and feel better, some of these same feelings were what made it really hard to talk about what had happened in the first place! From what I understand, these difficult feelings are very common and to be expected. It is sometimes really hard to know what you are feeling or why (sometimes all I know is that I feel really screwed up but I do not know why and cannot put a label on it), so reading this next bit might give you a clue to what you could be feeling too, if anything similar has happened to you.

Embarrassment

Talking about what happened to me meant I had to say words that I am not comfortable saying and discuss things that society usually keeps private. Feeling embarrassed is very normal in this kind of situation, and everyone (not just us Aspies) would feel that. Ultimately, we need our society to change its attitude to become one in which people are more open and honest about sex, sexual abuse and rape. Failing to be open and honest about these things is making it very difficult, quite unnecessarily, for loads of women and girls to report abuses, and is therefore protecting sexual abusers, helping them to escape justice and to carry on abusing people. If everyone talked about these things more, we would all feel much less embarrassed. However, until this point, we will just need to be brave and to not let our embarrassment stop us from talking about what happened.

Fear and anxiety

Because I felt so very embarrassed, I was very afraid to say anything to anyone. It took a lot of courage to do that. However, if you do not tell anyone, no-one can help you, and you are locked in a prison of a private horror of your very own. I decided that overcoming my fear would be better than sitting alone with that horror. I chose the safest person that I know to talk to about this. This meant that although I still felt very, very scared, some part of me knew that I was safe to tell her.

Part of my fear came from being very aware that I am different to most other people and very aware how what I am saying could so very easily be misunderstood by a non-spectrum person. Aspie girls are not slutty people, we really are not. We are probably some of the least slutty people in the world. However, I was rather concerned that some of my behaviour might look like sluttiness, whereas it was actually more a lack of knowledge and lack of skill; an inability to understand and say 'no' rather than a wish to say 'yes'. I have a lot of experience of my behaviour being misinterpreted, with people not properly understanding my reasons for doing something.

The good news is that many non-spectrum people are certainly capable of understanding, but they may need to use empathy and imagination to see where we are coming from. This is especially true if the thing that we just did not know or understand was something that most people would find obvious without having to be told. For the same reasons, I was also afraid about what people would think of me for having written what I have done in this book. The only person that I was not afraid of reading my first draft was one of my Aspie friends. I knew she would instantly, intuitively understand, whereas my non-spectrum readers would need empathy and imagination for an Aspie viewpoint.

If you feel scared like me, that is perfectly alright and understandable, but it does not mean that you should give in to the fear. However, it does mean that you need to be very careful who you choose to tell. And it also means you might have to use a lot of words to explain to them what you thought, and why, and what your knowledge and skills were at the time. Do not assume that they automatically know. Many non-spectrum people are blessed with an abundance of empathy and imagination, which is a fantastic gift to us. You just need to find the best one that you can. We are very good at finding the right people. We have good instincts as to who we need and who is safe for us.

Guilt

I felt guilty because I had not managed to understand what was happening at first and that it was wrong, and then when I did understand, I did not manage to say 'no', either verbally or non-verbally, and I did absolutely nothing to stop it happening. I felt stupid, weak and cowardly.

Actually, I did not need to feel guilty for these things. I was not weak or cowardly, I just did not have the understanding about what was right and wrong; the knowledge; the ability to say 'no' to protect my boundaries or even to know what boundaries were; the life experience to respond in any other way at the time; or any means of escape. I was not stupid, I was just vulnerable and innocent. Also, I have since learned that a 'freezing' reaction is quite common in a traumatic situation. This is the body trying to protect you from harm. For example, not resisting might make the other person less likely to harm you.

I also felt guilty because I actually liked some of it. I liked being touched and stroked. It felt pleasant, gentle, tender, nice and safe. I have since learned that lots of people who have been sexually abused or raped feel guilty for similar reasons.

I explained in Chapter 5 how people who are sexually abused often experience sexual pleasure, including orgasms, during the abuse, because these are automatic body responses that are triggered by touch. The experience of being sexually abused typically causes conflicting feelings, which may include pleasure, wanting it, not wanting it, fear, pain, hate, self-hate, guilt, shame, and confusion due to having all these mixed up and contradictory feelings. Since brains are programmed to seek pleasure, some people may unwittingly ask for a sensory experience to be repeated, perhaps without recognising it as being sexual.

If this has ever happened to you, at any age, I am so sorry. My heart is breaking for you. The first thing you need to know is this was not your fault and you are not guilty. *Not guilty*. Whatever you did or whatever you did not do. Whatever you felt. However you reacted. Even if you asked for it to happen again or sought it out again – this was the effect of the manipulation and was not your fault. Children cannot ask for or want sex unless they are abused first; it is against nature, and although children do explore their bodies, and experience pleasurable sensations, they are not usually seeking an orgasm. Also, no-one, at any age, wants to be sexually abused. Any pleasure you might have experienced was due to manipulation, and any thoughts or statements that you wanted the abuse are lies. You are not guilty.

The truth is that if you have been sexually abused, any sexual pleasure you experienced was not your fault. Your body just responded in the way that *all* female bodies do, because of an evil act by someone else that you could not control. The feelings of pleasure are irrelevant because they were caused by a mechanical body response which was outside of your control. You did not want the abuse, you are not responsible for it and you have nothing to feel guilty or ashamed about.

My feelings of guilt made it harder for me to tell anyone what had happened to me – I had none of this knowledge at the time. But I still had to talk about it in order to see the situation more clearly and to end up not feeling guilty about it anymore.

Shame

I felt that I must be a bad person because I did not manage to object or stop it happening. Feeling ashamed made it harder to tell anyone what had happened. Actually, I do not need to feel ashamed because I am not a bad person and I did the best that I could at the time with the knowledge that I had.

So, if you are in a similar situation, what to tell yourself is that the evil is all on the man's part, not yours, so the guilt and shame properly belongs to him, not to you. Since anyone can get sexually abused, you were mostly just unlucky, and the shame and embarrassment does not belong to you and is not justified. It is not always possible to protect yourself from abuse, even if you know all the rules and even if you act perfectly, sensibly, intelligently and with great skill.

You still do not need to feel guilty or ashamed, even if you have not managed to be all that sensible, as I often am not. I get lost easily, and once ended up in the red light district of a city by accident at one o'clock in the morning when I came out of a nightclub and walked in the wrong direction. I am also drawn towards quieter places like alleys and parks in the evening, I have a really low awareness of danger, I cannot see people's hidden motives and I cannot tell very well who is dangerous from who is nice…well, you get the idea. Not very sensible behaviour combined with a low skill for keeping myself safe: this makes me very vulnerable. These are all very typical Aspie traits, so you might find this stuff hard too. But none of this is badness on my part; it is just me being vulnerable and struggling to get stuff right. Guilt and shame are only deserved by people who have done evil, not for people who did their best but just made a few mistakes because they are vulnerable.

3. Forgive yourself

It is really important that you forgive yourself for anything you feel you did that contributed to any part of the situation, even if it was just that you made a mistake by trusting the wrong person, or that you went to the wrong place at the wrong time. It is really important that you do not berate yourself over and over for anything that you did.

It is okay to make mistakes.

Do not feel too bad if you did not manage to prevent something bad happening to you because you were not able to think fast enough or work out what to do. These are really hard things to do. Not being able to understand a situation, to say 'no', push the person away or be able to stop someone doing something you did not want, is not the same thing as actually consenting for this to happen. So, you do not have to feel ashamed.

A good life philosophy is that you can only work with what you know at the time. When you learn more in the future, you can act with a different understanding. But before you understand something properly, when you are innocent and naive, when other people have not given you any clear information and guidelines or rules, and when you are quite possibly without the support structures in your life that a lot of other people have, it is quite normal to make mistakes.

When I managed to tell my safe person what had happened to me, she was very kind and she did not reject me or judge me. Because she did not reject me, I felt less inclined to reject myself and more able to forgive myself. I stopped feeling guilty and ashamed. The memory stopped bothering me. Now it is just a memory, like any other, and not something that is going to traumatise me anymore.

4. Be angry!

I was very surprised to find this on the list. I always thought that anger was a bad thing and nice girls were not supposed to be angry. However, anger is a very natural emotion and has important purposes. For instance, if someone behaves unfairly to you, it is a good response to feel angry. If someone kicks you on purpose, the appropriate emotional response is anger and not happiness. If you did not feel angry, then you would not take any preventative action, and it would happen again and again. Anger, properly channelled, can cause you to take good actions to protect yourself and others.

With all emotions, we cannot actually help whether we feel them or not. What we can do is control our response to the emotions (which will then affect how long we continue to feel the emotions). So, with anger, you cannot help actually getting angry in the first place. But you can control what you do in response to your anger.

So, when something bad happens to me, if I think, 'I am a good girl, good girls do not get angry, I have no anger about this,' I am actually deceiving myself. Instead of getting rid of the anger, I have pushed my anger outside of my conscious awareness, but it is still there inside me, affecting my subconscious and my mental and physical health. This is not a good situation.

If you have had any dodgy experiences with a man who was not your boyfriend, or any abusive sexual experiences that you did not want but could not stop, remember that however you managed to act or did not act, you are not primarily the one at fault. You might not have understood what was going on or the implications at the time. But the man you were with certainly did. He is the one primarily at fault and it is normal to feel angry at him.

Anger is, however, a tricky emotion for anyone to handle skilfully and a few things are very important:

- Although it is normal, natural and perfectly okay to get angry when bad things happen to you, you do not want to get stuck forever in an angry state. This is called bitterness and it will rob you of your joy in life, make you ill and affect your relationships with other people.

- Whilst you are feeling angry, it is very easy to react badly against the world in general, even totally innocent bystanders who have nothing to do with the cause of your anger. Try your best not to do anything when you are in this highly emotional state that will hurt other people.

- In order not to get stuck in an angry state forever, you first need to get rid of your anger. You do this by acknowledging your anger (not denying it exists), properly feeling it and then expressing it. Expressing your anger lets it out of your body and mind, so that your anger is not trapped within you anymore.

- In choosing a way to express your anger, find a way that will not cause your anger to hurt other people.

- Positive ways to express and let out your anger include punching a cushion, going far away from people and shouting a lot, and writing a letter to the person who abused you, not sending it, and burning it or destroying it in another manner. The act of writing is enough. This exercise is nothing to do with communicating with your abuser (probably a bad plan and not safe for you). The act of writing gets your emotions down on paper and out of your head, and that is the important bit.

After expressing your anger (in other words, getting it out of your system), you need to forgive the person who hurt you (step 5).

5. Forgive the other person (but do not forget)

Okay, please do not think I am off my rocker here, but forgiveness is really important. Whether you have been hurt in a big way or a small way, by accident or on purpose, if you want to be truly free of the situation and the pain it has caused you, I believe that the only way is to forgive the person who has hurt you.

Some people have not yet learned this and they believe that they should not forgive people who have hurt them, particularly if they have been hurt very badly. This is a pity. I cannot prove to you that forgiveness is right and these other people are wrong. But I can tell you that the people I know who hold unforgiveness in their hearts and who bear eternal grudges against the people who have hurt them are also the unhappiest people I know.

There are three common misunderstandings about forgiveness, which I will now clear up:

1. Forgiveness does not mean saying that what happened to you was okay. It just means cancelling a debt, ceasing to want to 'get your own back' for what they did to you, stopping wanting anything from them (even if it is just an apology or an acknowledgement that they hurt you) and releasing yourself, more than anything, from the chains that bind you to the person who hurt you. Forgiveness is something that primarily helps you, not the other person. In contrast, refusing to forgive does not harm the person you are refusing to forgive. Refusing to forgive does, however, greatly harm yourself. Refusing to forgive is an excellent way to keep your anger and bitterness locked up inside you forever, poisoning you from the inside and preventing you being truly happy in your life. I heard someone say that unforgiveness is like trying to poison someone else, but instead drinking the poison yourself. This is completely right.

2. There is a common phrase 'forgive and forget', but this is very misleading because the two things do not go together. Some people think forgiveness must be wrong because they cannot forget. But forgiveness does not mean that you have to forget what happened to you. In contrast, forgetting would be a very bad thing. We learn by our experiences, the bad ones as well as the good. If we forgot what happened to us, we could not learn by it, and it would most likely happen again. I read about a woman who had been sexually abused by her father. She suppressed the memory and genuinely did not remember it for years. Then, her own daughter got abused by her father in the same way. The woman thought she was supposed to 'forgive and forget'. But by forgetting, she failed to protect her daughter. A terrible result. Forgiveness just means that you give up your desire for revenge on the person that hurt you, but it does not mean that you should forget or fail to take any

steps to protect yourself, or your loved ones, from that person in the future.

3. Forgiveness does not mean that you necessarily ever have to trust the person again, be reconciled to them, ever see them again, or be their friend. You can forgive someone who never actually knows that you have forgiven them. You can forgive someone who is dead. Forgiveness and reconciliation are two completely different things. Sometimes it is safe to reconcile, but sometimes it is not safe. It is only potentially okay to reconcile if the other person is genuinely sorry for what they did and you have proof that they have changed and will never act in that way again. But, it is always a good plan to forgive.

Forgiveness is a very good habit to get into, because forgiveness sets you free. This applies for the little wrongs done to you in your life as well as the big ones, and is an ongoing discipline because people hurt each other all the time. It might be easiest to start with forgiving trivial issues and then move on to the bigger ones. I find forgiveness can be really hard and I might need help from other people with this if I am still in a state of mental trauma about a situation. However, I do really see the sense in forgiving, and I have seen the devastation and the illness that results in my life if I do not do it. The only sensible choice is to forgive, however much I may not want to do it. Some things are harder for me to forgive than others, and for me, it mainly depends on what I perceive the other person's motive to be. Some people hurt me by accident – for example, they genuinely misunderstood my communication, thought I was being disrespectful and that is why they shouted at me. These people are easiest to forgive. Other people hurt me because they meant to. These people are harder for me to forgive. But this does not ultimately matter. The only sensible choice is to forgive everyone, for either type of hurt.

I found that when I have got through steps 1 to 4 above then the forgiving step is much easier. However, trying to forgive someone whilst I am still in a state of immense anger and hurt, I have found to be impossible. I might especially need someone else to help me to deal with my anger and hurt. Dealing first with the anger and hurt and any emotional upheaval seems to be important to do before the forgiveness step can really be done effectively.

Ways to forgive

How do you forgive people? This is a matter of style and does not matter as long as you do genuinely forgive them in your heart and you are not just pretending that you do. Here are some suggestions:

- Get someone wise to help you with it. They can speak out the words if you want, as long as you agree with them in your heart.

- Speak it out yourself, and mean it. It is no good if you do not mean it.

I prefer to have someone who is good at forgiveness to help me. But I can do it by myself. When I do not have anyone to help me, I do forgiveness this way:

1. I lie down on the floor, flat on my stomach, in a room where I am alone and will not be interrupted or overheard.

2. I relax all the muscles in my body, starting from the feet and working my way upwards.

3. When I am feeling really relaxed, warm and safe, I recall the experience that is bothering me and the person I am wanting to forgive. I use a very gentle voice and speak about the incident that is bothering me and the person it happened with.

4. If there is any excuse or reason for the behaviour that hurt me, I speak about this (sometimes there is no excuse or reason if it is an act of evil).

5. I say that I hope the person learns from the experience, avoids such behaviour in the future, finds some morals, or learns to be a better person.

6. I imagine myself having been connected to them by a chain. I imagine the chain representing a connection by which things from me have passed to the other person and vice versa. I mentally return everything that was transmitted from me to them, back to me. I mentally return everything they have transmitted to me, back to them.

7. I imagine breaking the chain so that we are no longer connected.

8. I imagine kissing them on both cheeks, I wish them well and imagine them gently floating away from me.

It has taken me a long time to be willing to forgive and to learn how to do this (with a bit of self-deception along the way, because I agreed with the concept of forgiveness a long time before I managed to actually do it for situations that really mattered, and yet I managed to convince myself that I had forgiven when I had not). But, I figured that locking up horrors inside of me was only going to add to my anxiety and make me ill, and that anything which could avoid this was worth a shot. Now I have done this, I mostly advocate it because of the result. I find that forgiving people gives me a tremendous sense of peace and finally does set me free and set my mind at rest.

Furthermore, we humans are curiously consistent creatures. How we treat others is how we treat ourselves. If I am critical towards other people, I find I am also critical towards myself. If I refuse to forgive other people for their mistakes, I find I also refuse to forgive myself for my own mistakes. In contrast, if I do forgive other people, I find I can much more easily forgive myself. Forgiving is therefore a form of love that we can give both to others and to ourselves. Forgiving says that we are allowing the possibility for others and ourselves to be imperfect and to make mistakes. I now think that loving oneself is tied up very closely with the practice of forgiveness, and that I have in the past simply been holding myself to unreasonably high standards of perfection because I have not, in fact, been operating with forgiveness.

CONCLUSION

Well, here we are. The end. Well done for reading this. It probably was not easy and I am so proud of you for having done it.

I am hoping that I have not made this all sound too scary. I am not wanting to put you off from ever having a boyfriend, and I am certainly not meaning to say that no men can be trusted. Most men are good and it is only a tiny minority who are bad. Relationships can be wonderful and very rewarding, and although this is such a difficult area, I believe it is worthwhile going through the confusing dating stage because of the potential rewards of ultimately gaining a family of our own. And Aspies can do it, even if some people assume that we cannot! Being on the spectrum has a strong genetic component, so clearly some Aspies are succeeding very well indeed in their romantic relationships, because that is how little Aspies are made…

One final rule: no worrying about any of this information! I just wrote this so that you are informed and prepared for what you might meet out there in the world, and so you can, all being well, feel secure in that knowledge. I hope that I have given you enough information so that you are able to protect yourself from things that you do not want and so that you can make your own, well-informed choices.

If some bad stuff has already happened to you, I am so sorry for everything you have suffered and for how unfair that was and I would like to give you a big hug. You are not alone. People love you and care about you. They would like to give you a big hug, too, and to help you with this, if you use your bravery to trust and confide in them. Know that everything is fixable and that you will be fine.

WHY THE ASPIE GIRL'S GUIDE IS WRITTEN AS IT IS

This section is for any Aspies who are interested in the thinking behind this book. It is also for parents, professionals, carers and for anyone who loves an Aspie. This might be particularly useful to non-spectrum people, to help them understand how to better communicate with Aspies.

I wrote *The Aspie Girl's Guide* in the only way that made sense to me to write it.

We Aspies start with the details and build up the big picture. I have written *The Aspie Girl's Guide* as a mass of details added together. My aim was for it to be a bit like a tree diagram, where branches represent different choices or situations, and to fill out every branch. For example, (A) is something which might happen, and you can then choose (B) or (C); if you choose to do (B), then be aware of (D), (E) and (F) and take action (G). (C) is a way of stopping (B) happening, which you might want to do because of (H) and (I) and if you choose (C) you would need to do action (J). I felt that it was really important to provide this level of detail, with all options filled out, to make the information as clear as possible.

Often, when I am given information, it is assumed that I have a lot of common sense and prior knowledge. This is all the more so in the field of sexuality, which most people are uncomfortable talking about. So, I tried to write this without assuming common sense or a lot of prior knowledge. It is really important to start from the basics. We Aspies are often not aware of what we do not understand – in which case, it is impossible for us to ask for clarification. We have taken in something, we do understand the literal words, so we assume that we have understood the entire meaning, when perhaps we have not. When in doubt, I choose to err on the side of caution and provide too much information rather than too little.

The Aspie Girl's Guide is explicit because we Aspies need things to be very, very clear. It attempts to cover lots of different situations, to say what is not allowed in various situations, to give enough information to make informed choices, and to teach specifically how to say 'no'.

One mistake people sometimes make with us is to give a negative instruction and think this constitutes a clear, useable explanation. It often does not. For example, someone told me: 'You don't have to French kiss someone if you don't want to,' but this was not nearly enough information. I could not act on this to alter my behaviour. A positive instruction as to what to do instead was needed, for example: 'If someone comes to kiss you, turn your cheek, so their kiss hits your cheek instead of your mouth.'

Many Aspies are great at following rules. However, where one rule (be polite or do not hit) contradicts another rule (push someone away to keep yourself safe), it can get confusing which rule to follow. So, I explained which rule was the most important, and situations in which it is okay to break other rules, for example, when it is okay to lie or tell a secret.

We Aspies sometimes find it hard to process things quickly enough to make good decisions on the spot, so I included lists of rules which can be memorised.

We may find it hard to understand other people's motives for their actions, so I have tried to explain what some of these motives could be.

We are not always good at understanding our feelings, or predicting what we might feel in a certain situation. For example, I was not able to predict how much I would feel scared by having an MRI (magnetic resonance imaging) scan or how much I would want someone with me afterwards – and because I had not predicted that, I had not organised anyone to be with me afterwards. So, I have described what people might feel in certain situations.

We instinctively believe that other people are telling the truth. I have explained that lying can sometimes be detected when you feel really confused because one set of statements seem to be contradicting another set of statements.

A lifetime of social confusion leads very easily to the belief that other people know much more about what is socially right than we do. My assumption is always that other people are behaving properly towards me. I am still frequently surprised to learn that someone else's behaviour towards me is wrong; in many different life situations, people can easily take advantage of me without me realising it. This means we really need to have the rules memorised, so that we are very sure of what is right and what is not. Usually, in life, you can manage by observing how other people act, assuming that is right and copying it, and that is generally what I do in social situations. But in sexual situations, this can lead you directly down the wrong path and into danger. It is vital that we understand this, or we will generally apply our rule of copying behaviour to these sexual situations, with bad consequences.

Some of this is very scary subject matter, so I tried to write it in a friendly and fluffy way, to take the edge off some of the scariness.

We Aspies are literal and logical. I have explained some of the words which are a bit confusing, non-literal and not quite what you would expect. For example, I explained that 'French kissing' is not the only way that French people kiss or something that only French people do, and that 'oral sex' is not anything to do with kissing.

A possible limitation with *The Aspie Girl's Guide* is that our academic IQ may be much higher than our performance IQ. You do need to be really high functioning to be able to apply this information well and skilfully enough in real-life situations. Some Aspies (and other spectrum people) may always need the rule 'never be on my own with a man' in order to be safe. Even though I have now researched and written all this, I cannot guarantee I will get things right the next time I am in a stressful situation, on overload and put on the spot to react in a certain way. Quite often, I do slip up over things that I actually know, if only I had a bit more time in the situation to access the knowledge and use it properly. However, there is a lot more chance of me (and anyone else) getting it right if we have this information first, than if we do not.

I wrote *The Aspie Girl's Guide* as clearly and simply as possible, from one Aspie to another. I did really try to write a stand-alone document. The subject matter is incredibly difficult and embarrassing for me to talk about and I am sure this will be the case for other Aspies too. I know everyone is a bit embarrassed to some extent, but I do get the feeling that my level of embarrassment is way higher than other people's, perhaps because:

- I have never talked about anything like this before, and other people probably have, at least in girly chats with their friends.
- I reckon many Aspies are emotionally hyper-sensitive, as well as hyper-sensitive to sensory input.

Reading something friendly on paper in the privacy of one's own bedroom is one thing. Discussing it with anyone else is quite another, and is much, much harder. So, I tried to be comprehensive and to write a book that would not need anyone else's interpretation, so that it can be read privately.

NOTE TO PROFESSIONALS

It was suggested to me that autism professionals might like to use this book to help support Aspies in this area. I applaud this motivation, and there could certainly be a role for professionals in giving people the information that we so desperately need in a really clear way.

However, please note the following:

- Even in a theoretical, classroom-like teaching situation, giving information on these topics could trigger memories of all sorts of past traumas.

- In a one-to-one support situation, disclosing personal things creates a bond. Disclosing things of a sexual nature which make you very embarrassed and vulnerable requires a huge amount of bravery and trust and creates an even deeper bond. However, the nature of your professional relationship might not permit this bond.

- In any situation with an Aspie, you are at risk of receiving 'too much information', even when you are not on such delicate topics. Some Aspies have truly horrendous experiences in their past; if they tell you about these, could you handle it? Would you know how to react?

- Can you avoid being critical or judgemental of the Aspie, whatever is said to you? Any critical comments would be exceedingly harmful.

- How permanent is your support situation? I have not been able to find any support for myself as an Aspie, from any autism or mental health service, which is not temporary in some way – for example, a block of six sessions of cognitive behavioural therapy, temporary post-diagnostic support, or a support centre dependent on short-term government funding. Every such support I have received, I have ultimately lost, but I am still an Aspie. I have found it devastating when support that I have been relying on comes to an end. The deeper the reliance, the more devastating it is when the support is taken away.

The way that my own trauma was fixed was with a lot of genuine love and gentleness. Saying something from within the depths of a hug where you are feeling safe and loved is different from saying it in other circumstances, and we Aspies do need a lot of gentleness, care and safety. I do not know what would have happened to me if I had tried to say what I did across a psychiatrist's desk.

I can only speak from my experience, and because of my experience, I would think the best way to deal with any traumatic situation is to do it within the context of a loving relationship, not a professional one. It therefore occurs to me that having a reliable, trusting and loving support network in the first place may be an essential starting point before you can safely broach the topics of sex and dating. As tempting as it might be to jump in with all guns blazing, sometimes you have to walk before you can run. I have spent most of my life not being able to deal with my traumas through the support network I needed not being there, and I suppose that was why I suppressed my bad memories. Now I have the right support network, healing can happen. I personally believe that making yourself vulnerable by disclosing these things requires love.

On the other hand, everyone is different, and some other people might feel more comfortable talking with a professional in a situation with a large amount of personal and emotional distance. If you are going to attempt to deal with any of this deeply personal stuff, I would advise that you be extremely clear, from the start, about the nature of your professional relationship and what it is, and what it is not. This may seem very obvious to you as a professional, as you have a contract of employment, and various rules regarding how you deal with your 'service users'. But it is very difficult for us Aspies to see social hierarchies, because we just do not think like this. From our point of view, Aspies are looking for supportive relationships. We have not been employed to use your service, and the professional–service-user hierarchy and rules may not be at all obvious. At least, they were not to me, and I felt like a complete idiot when I eventually figured out, after more than a year, that autism professionals are not 'friends'. So, I am not saying do not attempt this work as an autism professional, but if you do, these are some things to bear in mind. Good luck and take good care of your precious Aspie!

REFERENCES

Australian Institute of Family Studies (2012) *Age of consent laws*. Accessed on 4 October, 2012 at www.aifs.gov.au/cfca/pubs/factsheets/a142090/index. html.

Canada Online (2012) *Age of consent*. Accessed on 4 October, 2012 at http:// canadaonline.about.com/od/canadianlaw/g/ageofconsent.htm.

Chapman, G. (1992) *The Five Love Languages*. Chicago: Northfield Publishing.

Cloud, H. and Townsend, J. (1992) *Boundaries*. Michigan: Zondervan.

Department of Justice Canada (2012) *Age of consent to sexual activity*. Accessed on 4 October, 2012 at www.justice.gc.ca/eng/dept-min/clp/faq.html.

NHS Choices (2010a) *What is an orgasm?* Accessed on 4 October, 2012 at www. nhs.uk/chq/Pages/1689.aspx?CategoryID=118&SubCategoryID=119.

NHS Choices (2010b) *What is oral sex?* Accessed on 4 October, 2012 at www. nhs.uk/chq/Pages/1685.aspx?CategoryID=118&SubCategoryID=119.

NHS Choices (2011a) *Sex activities and risk*. Accessed on 4 October, 2012 at www.nhs.uk/livewell/stis/pages/sexualactivitiesandrisk.aspx.

NHS Choices (2011b) *Sexually transmitted infections (STIs)*. Accessed on 4 October, 2012 at www.nhs.uk/conditions/Sexually-transmitted-infections/ Pages/Introduction.aspx.

NHS Choices (2011c) *Contraception*. Accessed on 4 October, 2012 at www.nhs. uk/Conditions/Contraception/Pages/Introduction.aspx.

NHS Choices (2011d) *Condoms*. Accessed on 4 October, 2012 at www.nhs.uk/ Livewell/Contraception/Pages/condoms.aspx.

NHS Choices (2011e) *Condom tips*. Accessed on 4 October, 2012 at www.nhs. uk/Livewell/Contraception/Pages/condomtips.aspx.

NSPCC factsheet (2012) *Legal Definition of a Child*. Accessed on 4 October, 2012 at www.nspcc.org.uk/inform/research/questions/definition_ of_a_child_wda59396.html.

Rape Crisis Centre Glasgow (undated) *If you have just been raped – or if you are with someone who has just been raped*. Accessed on 4 October, 2012 at www. rapecrisiscentre-glasgow.co.uk/index.php?id=196.

Rape Crisis Scotland (2010) *Working to end sexual violence*. Accessed on 4 October, 2012 at www.rapecrisisscotland.org.uk/help/information.

RESOURCES

United Kingdom
Emotional Health
CHILDLINE
www.childline.org.uk
Helpline: 0800 1111

SAMARITANS
www.samaritans.org.uk
Helpline: 08457 90 90 90 (UK); 1850 60 90 90 (international)

WOMEN'S REFUGE
http://refuge.org.uk
Helpline: 0808 2000 247

YOUNG MINDS
www.youngminds.org.uk
Helpline: 020 7089 5050

Sex, Sexual Health and Pregnancy
BRITISH ASSOCIATION FOR ADOPTION AND FOSTERING
http://baaf.org.uk
Helpline: 020 7421 2600

BROOK
www.brook.org.uk
Helpline: 0808 802 1234

CARE CONFIDENTIAL
www.careconfidential.com
Helpline: 0300 4000 999

172 The Aspie Girl's Guide to Being Safe with Men

FAMILY PLANNING ASSOCIATION
www.fpa.org.uk
Helpline: 0845 122 8690 (UK); 0845 122 8687 (Northern Ireland)

Sexual Abuse

METROPOLITAN POLICE
www.met.police.uk

RAPE CRISIS (ENGLAND AND WALES)
www.rapecrisis.org.uk
Helpline: 0808 802 9999 (12noon–2.30pm and 7pm–9.30pm)

RAPE CRISIS (SCOTLAND)
www.rapecrisisscotland.org.uk
Helpline: 08088 01 03 02 (6pm–12midnight)

United States
Emotional Health

CONTACT USA
www.contact-usa.org
Helpline: 1-800-273-8255

Sex, Sexual Health and Pregnancy

PLANNED PARENTHOOD
www.plannedparenthood.org
Helpline: 1-800-230-7526

Sexual Abuse

RAINN (RAPE, ABUSE AND INCEST NATIONAL NETWORK)
www.rainn.org
Helpline: 1-800-656-4673

Australia
Emotional Health
SAMARITANS AUSTRALIA
www.samaritans.org.au

Sex, Sexual Health and Pregnancy
SEXUAL HEALTH AND FAMILY PLANNING AUSTRALIA
www.shfpa.org.au

Sexual Abuse
1800RESPECT NATIONAL SEXUAL ASSAULT, DOMESTIC FAMILY VIOLENCE COUNSELLING SERVICE
www.1800respect.org.au
Helpline: 1800-737-732

Canada
Emotional Health
BEFRIENDERS WORLDWIDE
www.befrienders.org/helplines/helplines.asp?c2=Canada

Sex, Sexual Health and Pregnancy
CANADIAN FEDERATION FOR SEXUAL HEALTH
www.cfsh.ca

THE CANADIAN WOMEN'S HEALTH NETWORK (CWHN)
www.cwhn.ca

Sexual Abuse
VANCOUVER RAPE RELIEF AND WOMEN'S SHELTER
www.rapereliefshelter.bc.ca
Helpline: 604-872-8212

ONTARIO COALITION OF RAPE CRISIS CENTRES
www.sexualassaultsupport.ca

INDEX